WICKED SISTERS

BY ALMA DE GROEN

CURRENCY PRESS
The performing arts publisher

GRIFFIN THEATRE COMPANY

CURRENT THEATRE SERIES

First published in 2003
by Currency Press Pty Ltd,
PO Box 2287, Strawberry Hills, NSW, 2012, Australia
enquiries@currency.com.au
www.currency.com.au

This revised edition first published in 2020 in association with Griffin Theatre Company

Typeset by Dean Nottle for Currency Press.
Printed by Fineline Print + Copy Services, Revesby, NSW.
Cover design by Alphabet.
Cover features Vanessa Downing; photo by Brett Boardman.

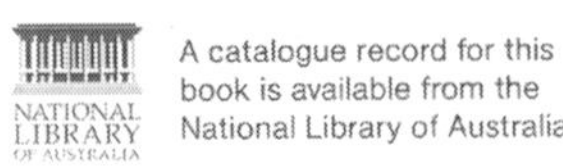

A catalogue record for this book is available from the National Library of Australia

Contents

INTRODUCTION

Wicked Sisters is a taut, tightly-written piece of theatre centred on a debate at the heart of contemporary political, social and personal convictions about moral and ethical behaviour. In less than two hours spent with four women in their fifties, Alma De Groen presents the issues surrounding the elevation of rational intelligence above imaginative intelligence and the effect this has on the way we try to ensure our personal survival. The play prompts the audience to think outwards from the predicament of this group of Australian middle-class friends to the global and national arena, where survival, security and prosperity tend to be seen as matters to be dealt with by rationalism and self-centredness.

The immediate situation on stage is so theatrically interesting that most of the audience will not spend the two hours extrapolating from the dilemma confronting Meridee, Judith, Lydia and Hester to national attempts to juggle economic or other modes of self-centred rationalism against thinking and behaviour which allow for compassion, generosity, sharing and altruism. The four women are enclosed in the disused study of Meridee's late husband, Alec, a mathematics scientist whose huge computer, still in use, almost dominates the room.

Alec Hobbes, a genius apparently of the Stephen Hawking order, but in his last years a victim of Alzheimer's deterioration, fell to his death from a favourite lookout while out walking with his wife. Although no charges were laid, the questions surrounding his death have driven Meridee into a reclusive existence broken only by frequent visits from her real estate agent friend, Lydia. Meridee, however, has invited a former friend, Judith More, a Public Relations consultant, for the weekend, and agreed to a visit from another friend, Hester Sherwood who, many years ago, was Alec's student and colleague.

As the play opens, Meridee leads Judith into the study with the words 'Hickory, dickory dock, the mouse ran up the clock', indicating the level of her husband's mental engagement towards the end. Alec was a complete rationalist, apparently deficient in emotional intelligence and creative empathy, with no belief in friendship, love or affection or anything beyond the mental and material. His computer is still monitored by university scientists who are interested in his project to evolve artificial life forms from random computer programs and observe the strategies they invent to survive—behaviours he believed to be necessary for the survival of life anywhere in the universe. As Hester says later: 'It's one of the dreams of science: to start from nothing and create organisms we'd consider intelligent. It was what he did with that dream that scared me.'

De Groen presents Alec as a Social Darwinist who believed 'that the weak would die out no matter what you did' and whose research and lines of enquiry were restricted by this conviction. To Hester, whose thinking was open to wider possibilities, Alec was a 'fundamentalist', whose intellectual acuity was blunted by a conviction that he knew the real, inevitable destiny of all living things, including ideas, beliefs and social institutions. The behaviours he observed in his simplified 'Critterworld' were, he thought, the behaviours that would be universally adopted.

We learn later that the program attributed solely to Alec was initially developed by Hester and appropriated by Alec whose pre-eminence established him as the final authority in the field of research he had created. When Hester's research questioned the limitations imposed by her mentor, it attracted no support because 'he set the agenda for what would be explored' and 'suddenly there was nothing for me to do'. Appealed to by Hester, Meridee chose to protect her husband and child and her own lifestyle.

The play touches here on an observed fact in the history of scientific knowledge commented on by the philosopher of Science, Thomas Kuhn: 'New ideas are only accepted when the defenders of the old die out (e.g. Einstein did not accept Quantum Mechanics: "God does not play dice with the Universe").' Alec had such confidence in war as the natural state of being that he added sound effects and gleeful predictions to announce that his 'critters' had reached that level.

Alec is named after the mathematician and utilitarian philosopher, Thomas Hobbes (1588–1679), whose understanding of human nature as essentially selfish in its drive for self-preservation nevertheless left him with a firm belief in moral, honourable and apparently unselfish conduct in civilised society. By contrast, Hobbes described the life of uncivilised man, in a state of nature, as 'solitary, poor, nasty, brutish and short'. During their brief encounter, Meridee, Judith and Lydia are shaken in their notions of survival as middle-class career women in the twenty-first century and realise that to preserve their concept of themselves as moral people they must sometimes act against their apparent rational interests.

It is possible to see Hester as the ethical centre of the play. Although pertinent questions are raised about her scheme for survival, as a catalyst for the others, she is essentially unchanged. The play leaves us with the thought that perhaps none of them are essentially changed, and that the shaky moral ground they occupy when we first meet them has been laid down by social conditions which they did not have the courage (or were not able) to resist. Possibly their notions of what it means to be in control of the 'real' necessities for survival have been questioned.

A number of recent plays include an after-the-funeral analysis of a famous figure, others centre on a reunion of old friends or family members, some involve attempts to raise money from wealthy friends, and others confront a wife with her husband's mistress. *Wicked Sisters* includes all of these themes in a compact plot, each supporting the central issue of morality in a rationalist society. There is not time here to consider why these situations have been dealt with so often in the last decades, but there are always sociological reasons why themes and plots tend to cluster during any period. Audiences and readers might like to consider if *Wicked Sisters*, for example, suggests any reasons for this phenomenon.

If Hester, a cutting-edge scientist herself, represents a stronghold of morality, it would be simplistic to see Alec as her opposite. It is true that he is afflicted with a condition, popularly described as 'emotional constipation', which is said to be more prevalent among men. Is he unable to feel emotions, as Meridee alleges, or has social conditioning and a limited view of success blocked his ability to experience and express important events in anything other than logical, rational ways?

He can certainly show the emotions of annoyance, impatience, anger and contempt, which are seldom rational responses. Even his summary of his dwindling intellectual grasp as 'the incredible shrinking brain' could be seen not as extraordinarily brave, as Meridee thinks, but as a form of bravado in a man unable to confront his own human tragedy. Alec is reasonably consistent (apart from showing petty emotions), and Hester's remark that they should at least 'give him the benefit of his moral indifference' is a reminder that consistency in self-serving matters is no virtue.

The play questions how many of us direct our lives as Alec did, and whether it is possible without someone like Meridee at our side, a person deeply capable of, and in need of, love and an emotional life. The denial of this need, cruelly driven home in her husband's last months, leads Meridee to kill the man who had effectively destroyed part of herself. Perhaps people like Alec, however intelligent and sophisticated they may be, are emotionally, in Hobbesian terms, 'Neanderthals' as Judith alleges. De Groen's later work has moved from a sometimes stringent feminist analysis of male and female relationships. *Wicked Sisters* may make even some women in the audience think more about the plight of Alec (and of the novelist George Johnston who is invoked in the play) than of the futures waiting for the women. At the end, we may feel as Hester says to Judith, 'You and Lydia: you're going to be fine'.

Wicked Sisters is alive with ironies, as is fitting in a play evoking the title of Shakespeare's Weird Sisters in *Macbeth*, whose double-edged prophecies set Macbeth on a path of destruction. Stage drama centred on moral issues can become a heavy theatrical meal, but the interplay of ironies prevents any danger of that in *Wicked Sisters*. An absurdly embarrassing situation experienced by many women passing through menopause is undercut by a neat reference to the discovery of Duncan's bloody corpse and Macduff's cry 'Horror! Horror! Horror!'. Several points are adroitly made without words, as when Lydia apparently absent-mindedly appropriates the expensive sunglasses from the handbag which she has criticised Hester for taking from the train. The sunglasses are perched on her head for the rest of the scene, silently emphasising the flexible nature of her idea of ethical behaviour.

It could be argued that there is little ambivalence about reason, logic and materialism; but empathy, morality and ethics are deeply complex issues. As Judith and Lydia move from self-satisfaction, despite a certain awareness that their initial moral stance is flawed, towards making decisions reflecting their more innate evaluation of themselves, the audience realises that they are still motivated by a sense of self-preservation. As Hobbes would argue, however, if they risk drowning by jumping into a river to save someone else because they have a sense of self that says they are altruistic beings, they are serving the ends of both reason and morality. No one has argued successfully that the race can be preserved without a measure of empathy in the human make-up.

Alec was not strong on empathy. Making a nice distinction between rational and emotional intelligence, Hester remarks, 'He may have been a genius, but anyone who thought artificial life forms were an adequate model for human behaviour wasn't exactly up there in the empathy stakes'. Empathy is the 'something Alec left out' that Hester intends to add to the program after she regains control of the project and it becomes her intellectual property. How she intends to do this in her program is beyond the limits of the play. All that matters dramatically is that her final words on the matter suggest hope, instead of the destruction dramatised by Alec's nuclear explosion. 'I don't know yet—that's the fun part. Feelings might be a good start. A strategy for world peace? Who knows?'

The question is real: who does know what might be done? There are enough unexpected developments in every part of global activity to warn us that the best intellect can never confidently predict what will happen. At a simpler level, Alec may have thought Judith would provide an ideal comfortable home for his child, but his lack of commitment to her and her belated awareness of how Meridee would feel, led her to frustrate his Darwinian plan.

Watching the behaviour of Alec's critters, Meridee suggests that Judith acted like those artificial life forms when she entered a relationship with her friend's husband: 'She knew what she was doing, but she didn't know why'. Unlike the critters, however, 'we can think about the consequences. We can think about our values', as Judith eventually did when she refused to have Alec's child. When Judith asks if Meridee thought about her own values when she pushed Alec over the cliff, Meridee admits 'I behaved like one of his critters—blindly. As one can.' The act, it could be argued in court, was not premeditated or malicious, but a 'survival' response to her belated understanding that Alec had suppressed her real self many years before his failing mind obliterated her and replaced her with the memory of his mistress, Judith.

This scene between Meridee and Judith is another key moment in the play's enactment of issues of morality and values. The tendency of women to feel and acknowledge guilt where it sometimes becomes more difficult for men to do so, often works against the expedient interests of both men and women. The women here do not wallow negatively in guilty feelings, but by the end of the play have reached a healthy compromise—or at least the best compromise we can expect in most situations—of acknowledging their mistakes, making recompense, and salvaging self-respect. That Meridee's 'mistake' is no less than manslaughter, and that the recompenses are extracted by blackmail, contribute to the ironic realism of the play.

Before Hester begins her blackmailing stratagem, after the failure of her attempt to raise money from the others to save their friend Rosie, she asserts 'Despite all evidence to the contrary, I still think we live in a moral universe, not a moral vacuum. Call me sentimental if you like.' She promptly proves she is not sentimental by manoeuvring the others into a position where she can get from them the money needed to buy a house and take Rosie away from the nursing home where she is rapidly turning into a vegetable.

There may be some point in Judith's accusation that if Hester had had any foresight in managing her affairs, she would have had a house ready for Rosie. The loss of property rights over the computer program and difficulty in reinstating herself in the academic world should not have daunted someone like Hester. Yet Judith herself feelingly recounts her experience of some months at the mercy of unemployment welfare after losing her job, and the reality is that Hester's occupation of cleaning motel rooms may be the best available. Judith's salary as a Public Relations officer in a multinational corporation is lavish, but she hates her work and its lack of moral values, and hates herself for doing it. The employment alternatives available to Judith and Hester summarise a dilemma facing a large part of the contemporary workforce.

An early draft of the play was titled *Through the Hoops*, and more importance was given to the difficulties of women and men facing the changes necessitated by middle age, especially changes in sexual expectations. The phrase 'through the hoops of middle age' is attributed to George Johnston whom the play sees as a sad exemplar of male weakness in this critical period, and his vulnerability is balanced by

Lydia's infatuation with the Ducati-riding thirty-year-old. If middle age retains any major importance as a factor in *Wicked Sisters*, it is because this time of life is an opportunity to assess and rethink one's values and lifestyle. It often requires some disruptive event to prompt that stock-taking and Alec's death and this meeting provide that shake-up.

Middle age is also a time when marital infidelities are most likely to be disclosed, or partners separate, sometimes before or after finding new attachments. Meridee has realised that the woman Alec addresses in his senile wanderings is Judith, and now wants to confront her with her betrayal. Ironically, she learns that Alec and Lydia also had a one-night liaison. Lydia's slightly melodramatic denunciation of Judith, 'You're the thing every wife dreads. You're disgusting…' is tempered by farce as Lydia has just confessed she was the woman retained in Alec's depleted memory bank.

Hester's active emotional and sexual life has left her without regrets, and in middle age she can advise the others that it is not imperative to desperately shore up the remnants of physical appearance and sexual activity. Unsatisfactory relationships in which, like Lydia, the woman deceives herself, are not necessarily better than nothing: 'Nothing is greatly underrated', says Hester. Hester has maintained an intellectual control over her scientific life although deprived of the means to pursue it, and middle age for her will be a resumption of research and experiment.

The underlying irony of the play is the ticking of a clock: who knows how long each of us will retain our intellectual hold on life? For some in the audience the chief dramatic concern will be the possibility that Alec's program too accurately predicts the fate of the human race. For others, it will be the possibility that anyone of us can lose our selfhood as a sentient rational being.

From the opening moment of the action, when Meridee indicates Alec's loss of reality, and reveals the phantom love world of his mind in his last months, *Wicked Sisters* almost teasingly alludes to the way in which our ideas of 'reality' deceive us. In some ways, most of us (and many would be proud to admit it) are fundamentalists like Alec and believe that in some matters we do possess the real facts or the real meaning. Yet the play does not encourage the notion that everything is relative. The firm moral centre is an imaginative understanding of the human effort to survive, an effort that requires empathy and sharing, and intelligent ethics rather than Darwinian competition.

If one of the main themes of *Wicked Sisters* is the elevation of rational intelligence over emotional intelligence and the necessity of balancing both if we are to survive as individuals and as a species, it suggests that our private exit from life may be coloured by sadness, irony or good humour without diminishing the value of our earlier life to others and ourselves. Life in twenty-first-century, middle-class, Western society may find many people, like the four women here, struggling to retain a sense of self-respect not wholly dependent on economic security. Hester believes that 'in their heart of hearts' people are altruistic. Perhaps it is a question of how much our altruism costs us.

The play does prove, however we interpret its action, that issues of ethics and morality are dramatically fascinating. It points up, by contrast, how dreary the political world becomes when expediency, rationalising and self-serving direct every decision and action. The late Bernard Williams, an outstanding moral philosopher of our time, remarked that a new way of being boring is 'by not discussing moral issues at all'. We might attempt to lighten the conversation with the issues raised in *Wicked Sisters* the next time our friends are discussing investments and real estate values.

Dr Elizabeth Perkins
Adjunct Professor of English
James Cook University
Townsville, Queensland

Dr Elizabeth Perkins passed away in 2004.

Wicked Sisters is dedicated to the real life 'Rosie', and her devoted friend.

Wicked Sisters was first performed by Griffin Theatre Company in association with Riverina Theatre Company at the SBW Stables Theatre, Sydney, on 5 April 2002 with the following cast:

MERIDEE	Judi Farr
LYDIA	Belinda Giblin
HESTER	Kris McQuade
JUDITH	Linden Wilkinson

Director, Kate Gaul
Designer, Kimm Kovac
Lighting, Stephen Hawker
Composer, Daryl Wallis
Sound, Aaron Symonds
Dramaturgy, Ros Horin and Anna Messariti

CHARACTERS

MERIDEE HOBBES

JUDITH MORE

LYDIA RENFREW

HESTER SHERWOOD

All the women are in their mid-50s.

SETTING

The Blue Mountains, New South Wales.

The late Alec Hobbes' study. Books are in the process of being sorted into packing crates. The half-empty shelves contain volumes by contemporary hard science writers. Any works of fiction are much less current. There are no papers or files that might suggest the study is in current use. There is a large, high-resolution monitor connected to a computer the size of a filing cabinet, which is plugged into a twelve-hour uninterruptable power supply. At no time do we see the computer screen, although the computer is on.

This is not a comfortable space, and during the course of the play the presence of the women turns it into a more hospitable environment.

TIME

The present. The play can be presented in two acts, or as a single scene with no interval.

Note: for the extinction event, Alec has put together a collage of sound effects from computer games including, very importantly, the fanfare.

ACT ONE

The room is in darkness except for a glow coming from the computer monitor. Two women stand in a spill of light from the hallway. MERIDEE *is pale and tense, dressed in sombre tones suggestive of subdued good taste.* JUDITH *is showy in a classy sort of way; she's generously built and gives an impression of well-groomed sleekness in a designer outfit.*

MERIDEE: 'Hickory dickory dock, the mouse ran up the clock.'

JUDITH: Nursery rhymes?

MERIDEE: That was the level of engagement at the end. There was the occasional lucid day when he knew where the toilet was and what it was for.

JUDITH: God.

MERIDEE: Not in this house. If he wanted to rethink his position on an afterlife it was too late. I haven't been in here in months.

JUDITH: Don't show me if it upsets you.

> MERIDEE *turns on a light, revealing half-empty bookshelves and packing crates on the floor.*

MERIDEE: People came from all over the world.

JUDITH: You must have been proud.

MERIDEE: I was always proud of Alec. Even in life.

JUDITH: His computer's still on.

MERIDEE: The university wants it kept running. They say anything happening on Alec's computer is more important than anything happening on theirs.

JUDITH: God, he was a clever man.

> JUDITH *takes in the impressive size of the computer.* MERIDEE *hits a key. The computer responds with an acknowledging chime from speakers around the room.*

MERIDEE: Alec enjoyed surround sound.

JUDITH: What's it doing?

MERIDEE: Evolving strategies for artificial life forms: things that life anywhere in the universe would have to do in order to survive.

JUDITH: What if you have a blackout?

MERIDEE: Someone from the Computer Science Department comes and boots it up and it goes back to where it was before the crash.

JUDITH: God, he was brilliant. [*Looking at the books*] Some of these would have to be first editions, wouldn't they? [*She picks out a book.*] George Johnston: *My Brother Jack*... [*Flicking through it*] Boy, what a marriage. I'm in a reading group: we read this book about Charmian Clift. The day after she committed suicide they were supposed to have lunch with friends. George rang and said Charmian had killed herself and would it be all right if he brought someone else? 'Couldn't make it through the hoops of middle age', he said. [*She replaces the book.*] I went right off George Johnston after that.

LYDIA: [*offstage*] Meridee?

MERIDEE: [*calling*] In here, Lydia. [*To* JUDITH] She has a key. She insists on being worried about me.

LYDIA *comes in laden with wine, and takeaway on a platter. She's small, fiery, self-absorbed, with expensive jewellery and a skirt defiantly short for her age.*

LYDIA: Sorry I'm late. [*She puts the wine and takeaway down. She sees* JUDITH.] Hey, my darling, give us a hug!

She and JUDITH *embrace.*

[*Prodding her*] You're *fat*, Judith!

JUDITH: You're dead, Lydia!

LYDIA: Is there a difference? [*Stepping back and twirling around for inspection*] How do I look?

JUDITH: Is that a skirt or a handkerchief?

LYDIA *turns to* MERIDEE.

LYDIA: I thought I'd never get away. I had to straighten out Skye— [*for* JUDITH*'s benefit*] she handles the rent roll. 'Look at my letterhead,' I said. 'It says "Lydia Renfrew Real Estate". I'm not running a drop-in centre for every down-and-out unemployed yobbo in the Mountains.' She makes them cups of tea. Just because I've put a Persian rug on the floor doesn't mean I welcome all comers. I'm trying to be a little bit special. [*Indicating the takeaway*] I got all your favourites.

MERIDEE: You needn't have worried about me, I'm not hungry.

LYDIA: I do worry about you.

MERIDEE: You can give me back the key.

LYDIA: I'm not giving you back the key.

JUDITH: Are we eating in here—?

MERIDEE: In Alec's room? Good idea, Judith. Why didn't I think of it? Alec would've enjoyed that.

MERIDEE *goes out.*

JUDITH: Is she all right?

LYDIA: There's still a lot of talk around the Mountains.

JUDITH: Must have been a nightmare for her.

LYDIA: It was amazing. You couldn't move for television vans. It's only a narrow street.

JUDITH: I saw you on CNN. You looked good.

LYDIA: Thank you.

JUDITH: You told the reporter they were a devoted couple.

LYDIA: They were. Meridee was *devoted* to Alec.

JUDITH: She's never confided in you?

LYDIA: Not a word. I thought she might have said something to you.

JUDITH: Just what a great funeral it was.

LYDIA: It was.

MERIDEE *returns.*

[*Louder*] It was a great funeral. Great.

MERIDEE *leaves plates, napkins and cutlery. She goes out again.*

You used to be so close.

JUDITH: Not anymore. Every time I rang and asked if she needed a shoulder to cry on, she'd shrug me off.

LYDIA: Why?

JUDITH: No idea. Then last week I rang, and suddenly it was: 'I've hardly seen you since you moved to Melbourne—why don't you come up for a little holiday?'

LYDIA: She's not on the Mountains A List anymore.

JUDITH: Surprised you're here then.

LYDIA: Bitch.

MERIDEE *comes in with a corkscrew and four glasses.* LYDIA *starts opening the wine and organising the food, very much at home, the family friend.*

Why have we got four glasses?

MERIDEE: Hester Sherwood.

LYDIA: Who?

MERIDEE: Hester Sherwood.

JUDITH: You invited *Hester?*

LYDIA: *Hester Sherwood?*

MERIDEE: She rang me out of the blue from Sydney. I tried to put her off, but she wouldn't take no for an answer. Said she was working two jobs—

LYDIA: Two jobs?

MERIDEE: And it was the only weekend she could get away. You remember what it was like: we were always pressured into something we weren't sure we wanted to be pressured into.

JUDITH: She had me outside Parliament House waving a coat-hanger and shouting about abortion rights.

MERIDEE: I got arrested.

LYDIA: She tried to stop me shaving my legs.

JUDITH: What does she want?

MERIDEE: She didn't say.

LYDIA: You didn't ask?

MERIDEE: She didn't offer.

LYDIA: You should have asked, Meridee.

MERIDEE: What? 'Haven't seen you in twenty-five years so what do you want now?'

JUDITH: But you were friends...

MERIDEE: We lost touch.

LYDIA: Good thing too.

JUDITH: [*amused*] You're not still scared of her, are you?

LYDIA: I wasn't scared! I couldn't stand the guilt trips. [*She hands out glasses of wine.*] She always made me feel as if we weren't doing our bit for the Sisterhood.

MERIDEE: We weren't.

LYDIA: 'Why does your I.Q. drop fifty points when a man appears, Lydia? Why is your hair that improbable colour? Your eyelids look like school ink. If you spent less time on your fingernails you could be out campaigning for rape crisis funding...' Well, we got that anyway, without me. What's she done since we left uni? I thought she'd be a famous scientist like Alec, or a famous feminist at least: Germaine Greer, or Gloria Steinem. She's not even controversial like—what's her name?—the fat one?

MERIDEE: Andrea Dworkin.

JUDITH: She was brilliant though. She ran rings round us when it came to brains.

LYDIA: I've done okay. So've you. That's a Prada handbag if I'm not mistaken.

JUDITH: You like?

LYDIA: Love it. Lose a few pounds and you'd pay for dressing, as my mother used to say.

JUDITH: How did we get to be friends? Remind me sometime.

MERIDEE: [*raising her glass*] What shall we drink to, girls?

LYDIA: To our friendship, of course.

They toast their friendship.

JUDITH: And to Alec.

They glance instinctively at the computer, then raise their glasses: 'To Alec'.

What a loss to the world.

There is an awkward pause. They glance uneasily at MERIDEE.

[*To* LYDIA] So how's 'Gotme'?

LYDIA: It was 'Got me Ferrari, got me apartment at Darling Harbour...' then it was 'Got me twenty-three-year-old waitress'.

JUDITH: What did you get?

LYDIA: I got the house and Choysa and Erin, except they're not living at home anymore. They spend a fortune, but I say, 'At least you're not wasting your money, you're buying clothes'.

JUDITH: You can't live with a man our age, they're Neanderthals.

MERIDEE: What have you got against Neanderthals?

JUDITH: Men our age are shits.

LYDIA: Exactly—!

JUDITH: Once I stopped putting all my energy into relationships I started to have a life.

MERIDEE: Reading groups?

LYDIA: I have to tell you, Judith—

JUDITH: What?

LYDIA: I've met this thirty-year-old. I'm in love!

JUDITH: You can't be in love.

LYDIA: Why can't I?

JUDITH: That's ridiculous.

LYDIA: I went guarantor for him for a loan. The bank manager thought I was his mother.

JUDITH: *He* probably thinks you're his mother.

LYDIA: Oh no he doesn't! Why are you being so negative?

JUDITH: I hate women making fools of themselves.

MERIDEE: What was the loan for?

LYDIA: A bike.

JUDITH: A bike?

LYDIA: A Ducati Monster. He takes me out on it.

JUDITH: Go, granny, go!

LYDIA: I feel twenty-five years younger.

JUDITH: You're not twenty-five years younger, he is.

LYDIA: Why are you being so mean? He's gorgeous.

JUDITH: What does he do?

LYDIA: This and that.

JUDITH: What?

LYDIA: Fixes things. He repaired my roof. That's how I met him.

JUDITH: What do you talk about?

LYDIA: We go to Eastern Creek Raceway… borrow videos…

MERIDEE: There are a lot of very bright handymen in the Mountains. They've all got economics degrees.

LYDIA: That's not Ramon. Though I'm pretty sure he finished high school.

JUDITH: What do Choysa and Erin think?

LYDIA: They rang all their friends and said, 'Listen to what our really cool mum's doing'.

JUDITH: What's the sex like?

LYDIA: I went on HRT.

MERIDEE: The things women do.

LYDIA: It was worth it. He's got the most beautiful dick—an aesthetic marvel.

JUDITH: [*to* MERIDEE] Have you met him?

LYDIA: I asked her to have a meal—the Grand View or the Hydro Majestic.

MERIDEE: That'd be fun: two old crows and a stupefying appendage.

JUDITH: I haven't had sex in five years.

LYDIA: You're kidding me?

JUDITH: I'll tell you when I've had a few drinks. [*She pours another.*] At one stage I got so desperate for human contact I started going to the dentist. He used to give me gas and stroke my arm.

LYDIA: What a creep.

JUDITH: He wasn't a creep, he was Californian. Then one day he says my gums are like his mother's and I stopped going.

LYDIA: I was in the health food shop and they asked if I had a Seniors Card.

JUDITH: They do that. They say, 'Now, how can I ruin this one's day?'

LYDIA: I went straight out and got my roots done.

JUDITH: [*to* MERIDEE] You know, you could take ten years off with a good cut and colour.

MERIDEE: What's the point?

JUDITH: I probably spend a quarter of my income on maintenance. People believe what they see.

LYDIA: [*up close and peering*] Have you…?

JUDITH: The lot. I'm practically an artificial life form.

LYDIA *lifts* JUDITH*'s hair and looks behind her ear.*

LYDIA: Good work, Judith.

JUDITH: The secret of a good lift is no one can tell it's been done.

MERIDEE: Then why have it?

LYDIA: [*patting her face and jaw-line worriedly*] I'm not in free fall yet, am I?

JUDITH: Wait that long and it's too late.

LYDIA: You think so?

JUDITH: I know so.

MERIDEE: I don't know what the two of you are going on about.

LYDIA: Think back, Meridee—

JUDITH: [*recalling*] Your fortieth birthday—

LYDIA: —we gave you a bloody great party—

JUDITH: —and you remembered you were thirty-nine.

LYDIA: You were such a drama queen about turning forty you were a year ahead of yourself.

MERIDEE: And then I realised how stupid I was being.

LYDIA: You can't give up. It's a war: you have to keep fighting!

She bangs her glass down beside the computer.

MERIDEE: Don't touch the keyboard!

LYDIA: Sorry! [*She moves back.*] What are you doing? Checking up on him? Secret e-mails or something?

MERIDEE: Why would I need to do that, Lydia?

LYDIA: Just wondered. I mean, it's on—

MERIDEE: It was never turned off. The university's still monitoring it.

LYDIA: Creepy. [*Looking more attentively at the hardware*] Pretty damn flash though.

MERIDEE: It's worth more than the house and land put together.

LYDIA: You're kidding me.

JUDITH: [*a little maudlin*] I really miss him… I really would have liked to talk to him again.

MERIDEE: Alec was a scientist. He had nothing to do with PR.

JUDITH: Everything's to do with PR.

LYDIA: You're not in some sort of trouble, are you, Judith?

JUDITH: Nothing I'm not getting thoroughly well paid for.

MERIDEE: Why is it always a woman explaining why we have to drive fifty kays because some phone company or bank doesn't want to give us any service anymore?

LYDIA: [*setting out smoked salmon*] Oh, God, do you think Hester's still a vegetarian?

JUDITH: I doubt if she's changed.

MERIDEE: At least she was vegetarian for the right reasons—ecological, not spiritual.

LYDIA: What do you mean?

MERIDEE: Alec didn't believe in a spirit: he said we don't even have a self, let alone a soul. Whatever the brain is doing, it's not doing it because there's anyone in there.

LYDIA: What do you mean, there's no one in there?

MERIDEE: We're a collection of stories that fool us into thinking there's a person there.

LYDIA: [*seizing her chance*] Oh, yeah? What's your story then, Meridee? Why are you still here?

JUDITH: [*warning*] Lydia…

LYDIA: It's a stunning house—I could probably sell it for you the first weekend it was on the market—but why are you hiding in it?

JUDITH: Leave her alone.

LYDIA: I've been wanting to ask this for months. Are you afraid of what people are saying about you?

MERIDEE: I don't give a stuff about people. Why should I care what they're saying?

LYDIA: Sitting here with a computer that can't be turned off—it's like Alec's ghost in there.

JUDITH: Lydia!

LYDIA: No, bugger it—!

The doorbell rings. MERIDEE *doesn't move. It rings again, longer.*

Well, it's not for me, Meridee.

MERIDEE *goes out.*

JUDITH: [*hissing*] What the hell are you doing?

LYDIA: We have to snap her out of it.

JUDITH: How many glasses have you had?

LYDIA: [*pouring more*] Not enough.

JUDITH: Well, go easy on it.

LYDIA: I bought the stuff, I'll drink it.

MERIDEE *returns with* HESTER SHERWOOD. HESTER*'s hair is a wild, grey mass, sparkling with raindrops, and she wears a man's overcoat several sizes too big for her. If she lay down in a park she'd be mistaken for a dero. She shakes her head unselfconsciously like a dog, raindrops spraying.*

HESTER: Got caught in the rain.

LYDIA: How did you get here?

HESTER: Walked.

MERIDEE: From the station.

JUDITH: In the dark?

LYDIA: That's miles!

MERIDEE: Didn't you bring a bag or something?

HESTER *has a handbag but no luggage. She puts her hands in her pockets and pulls out a toothbrush from one and a pair of knickers from the other.*

HESTER: [*cheerfully*] All here.

She stuffs them back in again. LYDIA *and* JUDITH *exchange disbelieving looks.*

MERIDEE: Take your coat off, Hester.

She fills the fourth glass. HESTER *removes her coat revealing leggings, a faded skirt and a mohair jumper honeycombed with holes.* MERIDEE *hands her the wine.* HESTER *looks attentively at her.*

HESTER: [*with concern*] How are you, love?

MERIDEE: I do things I haven't done in years: read all night in bed, play the radio all day—

HESTER: Giving the mind some healing time.

MERIDEE: [*unsettled*] Probably.

HESTER: I saw a tour bus when I was coming along, stopped at the Leura lights. It was full of women our age. I saw this beautiful face pressed to the glass, like a mask of sorrow… an ancient, ancient sorrow… Etruscan, Greek… staring out of the window of a Cobb & Co bus…

LYDIA: You should have got a taxi. You could have rung. One of us would have come and got you.

HESTER: [*to* MERIDEE] Are you taking proper care of yourself? Are you sleeping?

MERIDEE: [*brittle*] Don't be nice to me, Hester. It's the last thing I need.

HESTER *desists. She takes in the room, the silence.*

HESTER: It's quiet in the Mountains. Alec would have liked that: a place to be quiet and enjoy one's own thoughts. There's no quiet in the city anymore.

JUDITH: Of course—you were one of Alec's graduate students—

HESTER: For a brief, heady time in my youth. We never saw eye to eye, but the nights of arguing were glorious.

JUDITH: Nights?

HESTER *moves closer to the computer.*

HESTER: Alec was a conventional A.I. man, top down, very solution-oriented. He liked to impose his will on the computer. I was a bottom up person: I liked to let things emerge—start with a situation of virtual randomness and let nature take its course. I said, if evolution worked so well for organisms, why couldn't it work with computer programs? We had some incendiary spats. [*She studies the screen.*] Who's taking care of it now?

MERIDEE: The university.

HESTER: Do they own any of it?

MERIDEE: He made them give up any claim on intellectual rights. They were so terrified he'd take himself off to MIT or Caltech they gave him whatever he wanted.

HESTER: So it's yours now. [*She stares covetously at the half-empty shelves.*] What are you doing with his books?

MERIDEE: The university's putting them in a special collection.

HESTER: If there's any going spare—

MERIDEE: His colleagues are sorting them out.

HESTER: I kept up with what he was writing over the years—mostly to have a good mental argument.

LYDIA: A good mental breakdown. I could never get past page one.

HESTER: It was bloody scary, seeing what developed.

JUDITH: What do you mean, scary?

HESTER: He started with nothing and came up with software that behaves with purpose—

LYDIA: Mine does that. It's trying to fuckin' ruin me—

HESTER: It's one of the dreams of science: to start from nothing and create organisms we'd consider intelligent. It was what he did with that dream that scared me. Alec truly believed it was a universal law that the weak would die out no matter what you did, and that his results proved it. He was such a fundamentalist I often thought it must have been difficult reminding him he wasn't God.

MERIDEE: Not difficult. Impossible.

HESTER: And now he's gone.

MERIDEE: Proving, in fact, he wasn't God.

There is an embarrassed silence.

LYDIA: What are you up to these days, Hester—apart from obsessing about Alec?

HESTER: At the moment I'm cleaning motel rooms.

LYDIA: [*stunned*] Really?

HESTER: I was lucky to break into it at my age.

JUDITH: But you've got a degree!

HESTER: There are women *PhDs* in Russia cleaning toilets.

LYDIA: This isn't Russia.

HESTER: Not yet.

JUDITH: What happened to your science career?

HESTER: It took a little detour down the Franklin River and turned Green. I write papers on bio-diversity. Corporations don't like them, and neither does Greenpeace.

LYDIA: [*eyeing* HESTER*'s clothes*] Didn't you save any money?

HESTER: No, but I saved the Franklin.

LYDIA: I mean since then?

HESTER: Most of what I earn goes on computer modelling.

LYDIA: You didn't become a celebrity feminist after all.

HESTER: Damn, I forgot.

LYDIA: Are you still involved?

HESTER: Yes, but it doesn't involve getting paid. Have you any idea how much money's been cut from women's groups in the last decades?

MERIDEE: It's a frightening way to live, Hester.

HESTER: Sometimes.

MERIDEE: The only security women have is money.

JUDITH: The only freedom.

LYDIA: The only fun.

HESTER: So far there's no charge on using my brain, and until that happens I'm not going to panic about things I don't have. There are books to read… ideas to explore—

LYDIA: [*pouring more wine*] To each her own.

HESTER *shivers.*

MERIDEE: [*remiss*] Are you cold?

HESTER: And a bit damp. [*She twists, trying to see the back of her skirt.*] I felt something tear getting off the train.

LYDIA: You've ripped the bum out of it.

MERIDEE: I'll find you some dry clothes. Come on.

MERIDEE *exits.*

HESTER: Try not to talk about me while I'm gone.

LYDIA: Why would we talk about you? I haven't seen Judith since she moved to Melbourne. What do you care, anyway?

HESTER: I don't. Just stirring.

HESTER *follows* MERIDEE.

LYDIA: [*as soon as they are out of earshot*] She looks like something the cat dragged in.

JUDITH: My cats wouldn't bother.

LYDIA: How could somebody get to that state?

JUDITH: There are a lot of people in a far worse state, Lydia. Don't you read the papers?

LYDIA: I mean someone we know. Or knew.

JUDITH *examines Hester's handbag, surprised.*

JUDITH: Good bag though… nice leather… too new for an op shop.

LYDIA: Show me.

JUDITH *passes her the bag.* LYDIA *opens it.*

JUDITH: *Hey!*

LYDIA: [*puzzled*] Nice wallet too.

JUDITH: Put it back!

LYDIA *puts the wallet back and puts the bag down.*

Missed your chance with Meridee.

LYDIA: Don't worry, I'll tackle her later.

She is peering in cupboards and drawers. She finds a bottle of expensive whisky, sees it's nearly full before replacing it.

JUDITH: You've got your eye on the house, haven't you?

LYDIA: She'd be better off in Sydney, away from local gossip.

The room is gradually becoming feminised: food laid out, scarves, bags, etc.

JUDITH: The place is immaculate. You could eat off the toilet.

LYDIA: Maybe that's what she's been doing.

JUDITH: What?

LYDIA: Cleaning.

JUDITH: Would you?

LYDIA: Yeah. I clean when I'm upset. Every bloody thing.

JUDITH: I eat. Every bloody thing.

She picks up her plate of food and moves to the computer.

LYDIA: When Gotme left, the whole place was sparkling.

JUDITH *moves the mouse.*

[*Worried*] What are you doing, Judith?

JUDITH: I thought it was a screensaver; turns out it wasn't.

LYDIA *goes over and looks at what* JUDITH *is looking at.*

LYDIA: What are those things?

JUDITH: Beats me.

LYDIA: All those weird little critter things?

JUDITH: Artificial life forms presumably.

LYDIA: Whatever they're doing they're doing it fuckin' fast.

JUDITH: Why were they at an unfenced lookout when he had Alzheimer's?

LYDIA: That's what everyone wondered.

JUDITH: But the police decided there wasn't a case.

LYDIA: They were pretty thorough.

JUDITH: But what did *you* think?

LYDIA: I think I would have been very tempted.

JUDITH: You're not Meridee.

LYDIA: No.

JUDITH: It's not in her nature.

LYDIA: No.

JUDITH: But I mean, how do we know it's not in her nature?

LYDIA: We don't know. Do you know what Michael did?

JUDITH: Michael?

LYDIA: Their son in Adelaide. The doctor.

JUDITH: Oh—Michael! What about him?

LYDIA: He's on his second marriage, right?

JUDITH: Right…?

LYDIA: And apparently that's not too woop. They've been living apart. Michael minds the kid on the odd weekend so the wife can get a break. One day he delivers the kid home, leaves it at the front door in its carry-cot, drives off, and rings her on his mobile to say the kid's outside. Didn't even know if she was home.

JUDITH: Was she?

LYDIA: Yeah, and bloody furious. I'd have ripped his heart out!

She gestures and inadvertently jolts the keyboard. The computer responds with a piercing alarm. They panic.

JUDITH: Shit, Lydia, what have you done?

LYDIA: I don't know!

JUDITH: Turn it off!

LYDIA: I don't know how!

JUDITH: Well, how did you turn it on?

The alarm continues in surround sound. MERIDEE *hurries in.*

MERIDEE: What are you doing? I told you not to touch anything!

She gets rid of the alarm.

LYDIA: Sorry.

JUDITH: I just moved the mouse—

LYDIA: I think I hit something.

MERIDEE: Don't touch *anything!*

JUDITH: Sorry. Is everything all right?

LYDIA: What are those little critter things?

MERIDEE: What little critter things?

LYDIA: *Those* little critter things. They look like drawings of twigs or insects.

MERIDEE: Mathematical possibilities that have been iterated into life forms.

LYDIA: Come again?

MERIDEE: Critters.

LYDIA: What are they doing?

MERIDEE: Evolving.

LYDIA: Is it some sort of game?

MERIDEE: It's not a game.

JUDITH: What do you mean, evolving?

MERIDEE: Going about their lives. They're born, they die, and in between they do the things we do: mate, breed, trade, make war—

LYDIA: Do they get old?

MERIDEE: If they're lucky; otherwise they get culled. If they haven't managed to gather enough resources they get out-competed by their offspring, or other rivals, and then starve and die.

LYDIA: Charming.

MERIDEE *is putting food on a plate.*

Good to see you're eating.

MERIDEE: This is for Hester.

JUDITH: Keep going. She looks like she hasn't had a decent meal in weeks.

LYDIA: Did you find out what she's doing here?

MERIDEE: We didn't get into that. You set off the alarm.

LYDIA: I'm sorry—okay?

MERIDEE: [*to* JUDITH] She took a jumper from your bag.

JUDITH: She went through my bag?

MERIDEE: It was open, Judith.

JUDITH: What the hell were you thinking of, letting her go through my bag? Fucking hell!

LYDIA: [*to* JUDITH] She always took Hester's side.

MERIDEE: Did I?

JUDITH: Bloody *cheek!*

MERIDEE: Is that how you remember it? I always took Hester's side?

LYDIA: Listen, Meridee, Judith and I are a bit concerned—you need to start getting out.

MERIDEE: Out where?

LYDIA: We're your friends, Meridee—

MERIDEE: Alec didn't believe in friendship.

LYDIA: We're not talking about Alec. You always quote Alec.

MERIDEE: He thought love and affection weren't real, just ideas that come and go—

LYDIA: Stuff Alec! [*She catches herself.*] Sorry. I didn't mean that.

JUDITH: You really think we don't care about you? Then what are we doing here?

MERIDEE: You rang me, and I invited you.

HESTER *comes in. She looks transformed. If she was comfortable in her skin wearing cast-offs, she looks absolutely easeful now; she has kept herself fit and there is a suppleness and spontaneity about her body language that the others have lost.*

LYDIA: [*startled*] Do we know you?

HESTER: [*amused*] I don't know. Do you?

LYDIA: You look amazing!

MERIDEE *hands* HESTER *the plate of food.*

HESTER: [*eyeing the table*] I see there's some smoked salmon…

MERIDEE: Would you like some?

She fetches it for her. JUDITH *and* LYDIA *exchange looks.* HESTER *eats with enjoyment.*

HESTER: Haven't had smoked salmon in years.

JUDITH: Spill anything on that jumper and I'll kill you.

MERIDEE: [*instantly*] Have some more!

She fetches more.

LYDIA: We were admiring your bag.

HESTER: Oh, yes. The bag. Let's have a look.

She holds out her hand. Puzzled, LYDIA *passes it to her.* HESTER *opens the bag and up-ends it. Out tumbles the wallet, along with sunglasses, a comb, handkerchief, a pen and a small, folding umbrella.*

[*Re the umbrella*] Damn… could have used that.

She opens the wallet, removes the money from it and tucks it in her bra. The women stare.

Someone left it on the train.

LYDIA: You're *stealing* it?

HESTER: Only the cash.

LYDIA: But that's—

HESTER: She looked like she could afford it.

JUDITH: How do you know?

HESTER *hands her the wallet.*

[*Examining it*] Louis Vuitton.

LYDIA *picks up the sunglasses.*

LYDIA: Fendi.

She tries them on.

MERIDEE: We'll have to ring the station master.

HESTER: [*amused*] It's a while since you travelled by train, Meridee.

MERIDEE: But there'll be someone we can ring.

HESTER: There aren't any keys, so she's not locked out. You can mail it back to her.

She puts everything back in the bag, minus the sunglasses, which LYDIA *retains.*

MERIDEE: But you're keeping the money?

HESTER: She can have her credit cards.

JUDITH: This is—

LYDIA: It's dishonest!

HESTER: How honest are you, my little chickadee?

LYDIA: [*the sunglasses are perched on her head*] Extremely honest.

HESTER: Meridee says you're in real estate.

LYDIA: Got my own business.

HESTER: And you've never told even the teeniest little fib?

LYDIA: Never!

HESTER: Never ever?

LYDIA: I've got two girls! Do you have any kids?

HESTER: Not that I recall, no.

LYDIA: I've got Choysa and Erin to think of.

HESTER: Not at home still, surely?

LYDIA: They never leave home. Not really. If you had kids you'd know that. All you're doing is looking after number one.

MERIDEE: Come on, that's enough. I'll post the damn bag back on Monday.

JUDITH: It'll get you out of the house.

MERIDEE: It'll get me out of the house.

LYDIA: Handbags are a dead give-away.

HESTER: They certainly are, let's see yours.

LYDIA: *No way!*

She scoops up the bag.

HESTER: Come on, I'm curious.

LYDIA: Bugger that for a joke!

She puts distance between herself and HESTER.

HESTER: There's something I want to see.

LYDIA: What?

JUDITH: She's not going to pinch your money, Lydia.

LYDIA: Wanna bet?

HESTER: You don't have to hand it over, just open it.

LYDIA: What for?

HESTER: Just something I want to see.

JUDITH: [*curious now herself*] Come on, Lydia, open it.

LYDIA *opens her bag and shows it around.*

HESTER: *Yes!*

She laughs.

LYDIA: You mean this?

She pulls out a sizeable plastic bag full of jewellery.

JUDITH: I can't believe you're still carting that stuff everywhere!

LYDIA: I'm not leaving them at home to be pinched. I've had some of these rings and things forever. Worth a shit-load of money now.

She removes some of the rings she's wearing and replaces them with others from the bag.

[*To* HESTER] Happy?

She holds up her fingers to study the effect. HESTER *shrugs and goes back to her food.*

So what did it prove?

HESTER: Possessions are a very powerful meme for you.

LYDIA: Powerful what?

HESTER: It's the same idea you had years ago, and it hasn't been displaced by anything new. I can't see you suddenly giving everything you've got to the poor, for instance.

LYDIA: [*offended*] I give to the Sallies, the Smith Family, buskers—

HESTER: That's a very powerful meme: 'Give to charity as long as it doesn't hurt you'.

LYDIA: We were having a good time until you arrived.

JUDITH: No we weren't, but we were working on it.

She starts to open another bottle.

HESTER: [*becoming sociable*] How's… what was it we used to call him?

LYDIA: Gotme's no longer with us.

HESTER *looks involuntarily at* MERIDEE. *Are there two widows in the room?*

HESTER: You mean he's—?

LYDIA: Died and gone to heaven—living with a twenty-three-year-old.

JUDITH: *Lydia's* living with a thirty-year-old.

LYDIA: I'm not living with him.

HESTER: Nothing wrong with a bit of inter-generational sex.

JUDITH: Where is he tonight?

LYDIA: Working on his bike at a mate's place.

JUDITH: A mate's place. Ah.

LYDIA: What's that supposed to mean? If he says that's where he is, that's where he is.

JUDITH: You can't trust someone that age. That's like believing your kids are where they say they are.

MERIDEE: As far as you're concerned, Judith, we can't trust anybody, young or old.

They all turn and stare at her, suddenly realising how silent she's been.

JUDITH: [*appalled*] God, do I sound like that?

LYDIA: Yes. You do.

JUDITH: I've got to get out of this job.

HESTER: What job?

JUDITH: No one trusts me, so I don't trust anyone either.

LYDIA: [*for* HESTER*'s benefit*] PR.

JUDITH: I go home after a day saying our people did everything right and the oil covering the harbour and turning the entire city into petrol sniffers is the fault of a foreign-owned vessel and its crew, and I eat myself silly. No one in the company likes me: I know every cover-up they were ever involved in, all their financial interests: how to marginalise and threaten them if they have an attack of conscience. I work long hours and there's no social life. I'm so lonely I think I give off a smell. People can smell it on me.

HESTER: Find something else.

JUDITH: Cleaning motel rooms?

MERIDEE: Ironic, isn't it? The women who fought for liberation seem to be worse off than the ones who only fought for equality.

JUDITH: I went to a Women's Health Centre for a massage. She asked how I was and I said, you know… I've been working hard, getting colds I can't get rid of, tired, not sleeping… Then she asked me something that absolutely floored me. She said, 'How's your spirit?' I didn't know what to say. Who asks that sort of question? 'How's your spirit?' What fucking spirit? [*She looks at* MERIDEE.] You said Alec didn't believe in a spirit, but, Jesus, if it isn't a spirit, what is it that's hurting so much?

Her face crumples. She puts her head in her hands. The others stare at her, frozen; then she looks up and laughs.

She gave me some drops! Fucking Bach flowers! Since then I've been tinkering round with Buddhism. I think it's calmed me down.

LYDIA *and* MERIDEE *exchange bemused glances: calmed?*

That's the great thing about Buddhism: you don't really have to do anything. I can't believe I drove all the way from Melbourne and dumped on you. But if not you… who? You're my best friends.

A silence. The others look at one another: are they?

LYDIA: [*putting it even more in doubt*] Of course we are…

She goes to JUDITH *and puts an arm around her and squeezes her in a hug.*

That's what friends are for—dumping on each other. It's great. I mean, nobody ever admits they're lonely. I think you're really brave, Judith. We're all in the same boat, but you admit it. You come right out and say it.

Silence.

I mean look at me: what am I doing with a thirty-year-old…?

HESTER: [*suggestively, trying to lighten the mood*] Yes, what are you doing with him, Lydia?

LYDIA: A lot of things I didn't do with Gotme.

HESTER: Such as…?

JUDITH *tops up her glass again.*

JUDITH: Five years ago I slept with this bloke—

LYDIA: Ah! 'Mr Five Years Ago'!

JUDITH: I shouldn't call him a bloke. He was too beautiful to be a bloke—

MERIDEE: First we've got beautiful dicks, now we've got beautiful blokes.

HESTER *looks puzzled.*

[*Enlightening her*] Lydia's has a beautiful dick.

JUDITH: He took me to an Italian restaurant. Nothing much to look at from the street. So anonymous you'd walk right past it. We went in and it was a whole other world. Obviously you had to be in the know. The best Italian food I've eaten outside Italy. And the wine! He ordered this buttery white that cost a fortune and tasted like heaven. I sat there thinking, 'Please let me get into bed with this man and not feel like a garbage bin next to him'. He was perfect: flat stomach, hair with just the right amount of grey, Armani suit straight from the cleaners—

LYDIA: Like one of those doctors in those miniseries that are always murdering their wives?

JUDITH: Exactly!

HESTER: Was there a brain attached to any of this?

JUDITH: He was a colleague.

HESTER: Debatable in that case.

LYDIA: Is this going anywhere?

JUDITH: Anyway, we go back to his place and it's—you know—wall-to-wall good taste. And we go to bed and the sex is great, no problems. Early next morning I wake up, and I'm lying there feeling pretty damn good about things, with him asleep beside me. Next thing I realise there's something sticky on my hands—

LYDIA: Sticky?

JUDITH: I lift up the covers and my hands are covered in blood. I've had a flooding in the night. Then I look at him. He's lying on his side with his back to me and his back and his buttocks are red with blood—

LYDIA: Oh, my God…!

JUDITH: —and all over his designer sheets. It looked like there'd been a murder. It looked like I'd killed him.

HESTER: What did you do?

JUDITH: I went in the bathroom and washed the blood off my hands and got dressed as quietly as I could—

LYDIA: He didn't wake up?

JUDITH: I wasn't waiting round for that. I let myself out, drove home, and faxed in my resignation.

LYDIA: You *what?*

HESTER: You resigned?

JUDITH: I couldn't face him. I didn't even go back to work. I said I was ill.

HESTER: So what? Menorrhagia.

JUDITH: I hadn't had a period in months. I was into the Change, I thought —and whoosh! A fucking flood.

MERIDEE: That was why you moved to Melbourne?

JUDITH: I had to. I was out of work for three months—with all the fun of trying to explain to Social Security why I'd quit my job.

They laugh.

HESTER: I wonder what he thought when he woke up.

MERIDEE: Horror! Horror! Horror!

HESTER: I wish I'd seen it!

JUDITH: I still see it. I have nightmares.

HESTER: Bet he does too.

LYDIA: Probably put him off for life.

JUDITH: It put *me* off.

HESTER: You care too much what people think, Judith.

LYDIA: It wasn't a love affair, was it?

JUDITH: No. I only fell in love once, and that was years ago.

LYDIA: I'm pretty sure I'm in love with Ramon. He's almost a different species from Gotme.

MERIDEE: He's a different generation.

LYDIA: His attitudes are completely different. It's almost as if he thinks I'm a person in my own right.

HESTER: If you're not one now, Lydia, I don't know when you will be.

LYDIA: I'm talking about what *he* thinks.

HESTER: I'm talking about what *you* think.

LYDIA: I was okay for a while—about a year after Gotme left. I was on my own and I was okay. I thought, why do I need a man? I was even enjoying myself. And then this incredible bloke appeared and I don't feel emotionally independent anymore. I want to know where he is all the time. [*She dials her mobile.*] He's supposed to be at my place when he finishes with the bike—

JUDITH: Okay, we get the picture: you've got sex, drugs and rock and roll, and you're in your fifties— [*She is tucking into bread and cheese.*] I shouldn't be eating this. I'm borderline diabetic.

MERIDEE: What about alcohol?

JUDITH: [*picking up her glass*] What about alcohol?

LYDIA*'s phone doesn't answer. She quietly puts it away.*

HESTER: You have to take care of yourself, Judith. We all do. Stay well, stay fit, stay happy.

LYDIA: [*remembering*] His sister! His sister has dyed blonde hair! I remember he said he was giving her a lift to her aromatherapy class!

JUDITH: Ramon?

LYDIA: I found a blonde hair in my bike helmet. He keeps a spare for me to use. I thought he had a girlfriend! [*Picking up her glass*] Oh, thank God, thank God!

JUDITH: You don't know it wasn't a bloke's.

LYDIA: I know hair colour—it was dyed.

JUDITH: I know plenty of men who dye their hair.

LYDIA: Not Ramon or his mates.

HESTER: [*appalled*] Is this worth it?

LYDIA: Well, I'm into it now, and I still think it's better than nothing.

HESTER: Nothing is greatly underrated.

JUDITH: [*to* HESTER] You'd be the expert presumably: are *you* happy?

HESTER: What do you mean?

JUDITH: 'Stay well, stay fit, stay happy.'

HESTER: I try and make a point of it.

LYDIA: You're cleaning motel rooms.

HESTER: So?

LYDIA: Look at the situation you're in. You can't be happy.

HESTER: What situation? My mum brought up three kids working as a cleaner.

LYDIA: How can I put this delicately…?

HESTER: I'll be interested to see.

LYDIA: You had more smarts than any of us, and where has it got you? I mean, look at me; look at Judith. Judith didn't just settle for any old career—

HESTER: No, she settled for deceiving the public.

JUDITH: Now, hang on a minute—!

HESTER: No doubt you have a politer way of putting it.

JUDITH: My first responsibility is to myself—

LYDIA: That's right. That's exactly right.

JUDITH: Taking proper care of myself, and not being a drain on the public purse. If you don't take care of yourself, how are you going to take care of anyone else?

HESTER: Who are you taking care of, Judith?

JUDITH: No one at present, but if the need arose, I could.

LYDIA: My father always said the best way to help the poor is not to become one of them.

JUDITH: Being on the dole for three months is as much as I ever want to experience in the way of a handout.

HESTER: You're both cheating other people, and Judith—by her own account—is bloody miserable.

LYDIA: And what do you do? Swab out the toilet bowls repeating, 'Life is beautiful'?

HESTER: You want to wake up, girls. Life can up and smack us on the arse. Look at Alec.

LYDIA: Alec was ten years older than us.

HESTER: It can happen at our age too.

JUDITH: It's a lot less likely.

HESTER: Is it?

LYDIA: There's a big difference between fifty-five and sixty-five.

HESTER: Do you remember Rosie?

LYDIA *looks blank.*

Rosemary Gordon.

LYDIA: [*trying to think*] Rosemary Gordon… Rosemary Gordon…

HESTER: You remember Rosie. She was a friend of ours at uni.

JUDITH: I remember. Piles of books all the time. She used to help me with my essays.

LYDIA: [*remembering*] Wispy hair and glasses!

MERIDEE: Wrote poetry, didn't she?

HESTER: She was a marvellous poet.

MERIDEE: Was?

HESTER: She's in a nursing home. She's had a stroke.

JUDITH: Oh, my God.

HESTER: One of those places where they tie them in their chairs.

LYDIA: Jesus.

HESTER: There's a woman in the bed on one side screaming, on the other side making noises like a crow—

She makes crow noises.

JUDITH: Oh, my God.

HESTER: They don't give her any physio and the ward smells of piss. You remember how fastidious she was. She cries all the time.

LYDIA: Oh, my God.

HESTER: The staff do their best but there aren't enough of them. Every time I see her she's more fragile. She's in hell, and she knows she's in hell, and my fear is… I think she's trying to starve herself to death.

There is an appalled silence.

If I could have her to live with me—

LYDIA: Surely she has family?

HESTER: Two daughters who don't give a rat's.

MERIDEE: *Could* you help her?

HESTER: I live in a shared household. She needs a place with wheelchair access, or the possibility of it.

LYDIA: A two-bedroom house.

HESTER: Up here somewhere.

MERIDEE: In the Mountains?

LYDIA: It's not as cheap as you might think. Not if you want to buy something close to shops and services.

HESTER: I thought the Mountains were still affordable.

LYDIA: Leura's expensive, especially South Leura. Katoomba might be possible. If you go further out it's cheaper. Do you have a car? No.

You don't have a car. That could be a problem. Public transport's hopeless unless you're on a direct route. You have to have a car.

HESTER: I don't.

LYDIA: I'm not sure I can help you. I'll keep an eye out of course. Does Rosie have any money?

HESTER: Not much.

LYDIA: I don't like your chances. I really don't. I don't think I can help you.

JUDITH: Public housing. Have you thought about that?

HESTER: She needs help now!

LYDIA: Are you and Rosie… you know?

HESTER: She's my best friend—not my lover.

LYDIA: Just wondered…

HESTER: [*looking at* MERIDEE] Alec was lucky he had you—you could keep him at home.

JUDITH: She was caring for a national treasure.

MERIDEE: If I was in any danger of forgetting it, Judith, there were plenty of people constantly reminding me.

JUDITH: He was on a level with Stephen Hawking.

MERIDEE: He didn't have ten nurses looking after him, just me.

LYDIA: *Ten nurses?* [*Thinking*] God, what would that have cost…?

JUDITH: Was he frightened?

MERIDEE: He was extraordinarily brave. 'The incredible shrinking brain', he called it.

JUDITH: What was it like?

MERIDEE: It wasn't anything much at first. He had this dark blue dressing-gown he'd had for years, and he said, 'This isn't my dressing-gown, it's somebody else's… It's not my dressing-gown. It doesn't fit.' One night we went to our favourite restaurant; they put his plate in front of him and he didn't know what it was for. He started to go out in the middle of the night to check the letterbox. On a sunny day he sat at the window and said, 'It's dark outside. There's a storm coming'.

LYDIA: Poor love.

MERIDEE: I'd read him something from the paper, and five minutes later he wouldn't remember what it was about.

LYDIA: God, I'm like that. I'm exactly like that.

JUDITH: Why didn't you ask us for help?

MERIDEE: Not every day was bad. There were times when he could think and function normally. We'd even go for walks.

LYDIA: The Lookout.

MERIDEE: The familiar's very important to Alzheimer's sufferers. Change upsets them. It was a special place for Alec—probably the reason we started to spend most of our time up here, although he never said. He'd go there whenever he had a problem he was working on. He said it was something about being high above things and being able to look down at clouds and trees below the escarpment. About seeing the inevitability of life, and how it continues to happen; like his life forms in the computer, going on mating, competing and evolving, even though the person who created them isn't here anymore.

JUDITH: He's not dead, Meridee.

MERIDEE: [*shaken from her thoughts*] What?

JUDITH: He's still here in this room, with all his wonderful ideas.

HESTER: What wonderful ideas? A billion people live in poverty because we think like Alec. Why do there have to be losers?

LYDIA: [*refilling glasses*] If there weren't losers, there wouldn't be any winners.

HESTER: He said competition leads to more interesting, complex and effective life forms; I agree with that, but if it was just a matter of competition, why would the woman who discovered medicinal herbs have shared them beyond her immediate family?

LYDIA: She got paid for it.

HESTER: From a genetic point of view, they were her deadly competitors. So there's more going on than just genetics.

LYDIA: And here I was hoping for a good old goss.

HESTER: In their heart of hearts I think people are more altruistic than that. Even those in this room.

MERIDEE: [*very tense, listening to* HESTER] People go on and on about science, but I don't think it's made us any better as human beings. Anything's permissible because people don't believe in anything.

HESTER: You mean in having a conscience?

> MERIDEE *gets up, goes to the cabinet and takes out the whisky and some glasses.*

MERIDEE: There's no morality now, only biology. We don't buy religion anymore, but what have we put in its place? Competition. That's what drives us, whether you like it or not.

She pours herself a whisky and gulps it down, not bothering to serve the others.

HESTER: [*watching her intently*] What's happening, Meridee?

LYDIA: We shouldn't have been talking about Alec. This isn't a wake. We had the wake. It was humungous.

MERIDEE: Alec was never a warm man. Never touchy-feely. I don't believe in all the years we were married he ever made me a cup of coffee. But Alzheimer's sufferers can be strangely affectionate. He was more… intimate… with me than he'd ever been in what I came to think of as 'real life'. He'd put his hand out and clasp mine… put an arm around me and nuzzle into my shoulder. One morning I woke up and he was awake before me, just lying quietly next to me. When he saw I was awake he put out his hand and touched mine. We held hands, just lying there, with the early morning sound of birds. I thought, 'Why wasn't it always like this? Why only now?' And then he said, quite lucidly and nostalgically, 'Do you remember Sibilla's? You said it was the best meal you ever ate.' He stroked my arm and said a name—not my name—another woman's. From that moment on I was erased from his memory. From somewhere in his past he'd produced someone else. That woman lived in our house every moment of every day until he died. She shared our kitchen, our bathroom, our bedroom and every last intimate indignity. She took my place completely. You know who you are. And I certainly know.

Three pairs of eyes stare at her in shock as the lights fade.

END OF ACT ONE

ACT TWO

LYDIA *has armed herself with whisky.*

LYDIA: I ran into him in Martin Place. I was going up and he was coming down. You don't want to hear this.

MERIDEE: Yes I do. I'm fascinated.

LYDIA: He was shopping for a new briefcase. I asked him if he'd like some help. We had dinner together. He said you were up in the Mountains.

MERIDEE: Did you use our flat?

LYDIA: No, of course not.

MERIDEE: Where did you go?

LYDIA: The Wentworth. I am so sorry, Meridee.

JUDITH: Bit late now.

HESTER: What got into you? Apart from Alec.

LYDIA: Gotme was grumpy because someone had dinged his Porsche that he had then, and it was before I had the girls—

JUDITH: [*aghast*] They're not Alec's—?

LYDIA: No way! They're Gotme's girls to their very bones. No, I think it was the weather—apart from the fact that Alec was so attractive in those days—

JUDITH: The *weather?*

LYDIA: It was one of those soft Sydney days we used to get years ago, when there weren't so many crowds, and not so much pollution—blue sky, a kind of relaxed, near-the-beach feeling, even when you're not near the beach… if you know what I mean. Anything seems possible and okay.

JUDITH: It wasn't okay, Lydia. Not at all okay.

LYDIA: [*to* MERIDEE] I am so sorry. It was the worst mistake of my life, apart from Gotme. If I could undo it I would. It wasn't anything. A blip on the radar screen. Just one encounter. But I'm amazed. I'm just astounded, that he remembered it all that time. [*Secretly chuffed by this*] It was years ago. [*She stops, puzzled.*] What I can't figure out though… you said he mentioned someone called Sibilla—

MERIDEE: You don't remember any Sibilla?

LYDIA: No, I don't. I honestly don't.

MERIDEE: I'm not surprised. Sibilla isn't a person, it's a restaurant. No doubt named after a person, but it's a restaurant.

LYDIA: Well, I'm sure we didn't eat there. Doesn't ring a bell at all.

MERIDEE: Where did you eat, just out of interest?

LYDIA: You know, I can't remember? I've got a hopeless memory these days. I don't know where we went, but I'm pretty sure we didn't go to Sibilla's.

MERIDEE: After meeting in Martin Place in Sydney and shopping for a briefcase I think it might have been rather difficult—given that Sibilla's is in Tivoli outside Rome.

Dead silence.

It took a while for the penny to drop. But considering I had a cookbook given me by Alec with recipes from famous Italian restaurants, and Sibilla's, which came up more and more frequently in conversation—if you could call it conversation—happened to be in it, the penny was bound to drop sometime. Sibilla's *'Conchiglie Ulpia'* you were particularly fond of. *'Conchiglie Ulpia'*: we had a fine old time with that one. Alzheimer's sufferers love to fix on a word or two and repeat them endlessly day and night: *'Conchiglie Ulpia'*. Pasta with spinach and rather a lot of cream. I looked it up. No wonder you're a borderline diabetic.

JUDITH: [*shaken*] He wasn't rational.

MERIDEE: I think he knew where he'd been, and with whom. He simply didn't know *me*.

LYDIA: [*stunned*] *Judith?* [*Looking at* MERIDEE, *dismayed*] You knew about me, though? Didn't you?

MERIDEE: No, as a matter of fact, I didn't know.

LYDIA: Oh, God.

HESTER: Please—I can't bear to be left out: I did try and mind-fuck him after his lectures.

JUDITH *takes the whisky bottle and pours herself a double.*

JUDITH: It was a long time ago, Meridee. A long, long time ago.

MERIDEE: You were working for a tobacco company. Lots of travel. Lots of conferences overseas. And of course, Alec was in demand everywhere. And I had Michael, who was in school. I think I could forgive the affair, which I suspect went on for some years, except that you took our last months together.

LYDIA: [*accusingly*] How long, Judith?

JUDITH: What's the point now?

LYDIA: *How long?*

JUDITH: Ten years.

LYDIA: You are *sick!*

JUDITH: Look who's talking!

LYDIA: One night, Judith! One night! You are so pathetic. Designer labels and you're still pitiful.

JUDITH: I wasn't then.

MERIDEE: No, you had it all.

LYDIA: We all had it all! We all had it all! And none of us has anything now!

HESTER: Did somebody just do a mass lobotomy? What happened?

JUDITH: I'm sorry. I'm so sorry.

MERIDEE: I had that routine from Lydia.

JUDITH: I care about you. Your friendship's important to me.

MERIDEE: You've been in the PR business too long.

JUDITH: You didn't get in touch with me for months—you didn't invite me to the funeral—

MERIDEE: People aren't invited to funerals.

JUDITH: I wrote, I e-mailed, I rang—you froze me out—

MERIDEE: Now you know why.

JUDITH: Then I rang and you said, come. You set me up. This whole bloody thing. You've been rubbing my nose in it ever since I got here: telling me he was reduced to nursery rhymes, 'Hickory dickory dock', and didn't know what the toilet was for—making us eat in here—I'm sorry about hurting you, but I'm not sorry about Alec. You didn't know what you had. You were such an upper North Shore princess—the right schools, parents with books in the house—

MERIDEE: You took my husband.

JUDITH: I didn't take him—he took me. That's the way it works.

LYDIA: Not always.

MERIDEE: I lost him twice, Judith. I lost the man I lived with, and I lost our past because of you.

JUDITH: Ever think there might be a reason for that? He loved me! And I loved him.

MERIDEE: If he said anything of the sort he was lying to you. Love was not in his lexicon.

HESTER: Unlike lying.

JUDITH: Just because you had a sterile marriage—

MERIDEE: It wasn't sterile.

JUDITH: No, you've got that sociopathic doctor for a son.

MERIDEE: It wasn't easy being Alec's son.

HESTER: Or his wife.

JUDITH: I had an abortion I bitterly regret.

MERIDEE: When?

JUDITH: When do you think?

MERIDEE: I took you to the clinic.

JUDITH: You did.

MERIDEE: What a validation you are. Alec must have been proud. He programmed things like you.

JUDITH *pours more whisky.*

LYDIA: [*to* HESTER] You know how lemurs fight? It was on this wildlife program: they see who can raise the worst stink. They don't try and physically maim each other, just asphyxiate.

MERIDEE: How can you justify yourself?

JUDITH: I loved Alec.

MERIDEE: He didn't believe in love.

JUDITH: Well, I bloody did! It was enough for both of us.

HESTER: He believed in the sexual drive.

JUDITH: How someone behaves speaks volumes, no matter what they say they believe.

MERIDEE: And how did Alec behave?

JUDITH: Like a man committed to a certain path.

MERIDEE: Which led to you.

JUDITH: Which led to me.

LYDIA: Sex! Sex, sex, sex!

JUDITH: I know the difference.

LYDIA: Hah!

JUDITH: Do you think I'd have gone through all that hell if I didn't?

MERIDEE: Was it hell?

JUDITH: Deceiving you?

MERIDEE: Then why do it?

JUDITH: No matter what I say you're going to howl me down.

LYDIA: He could have had anyone. He was an international figure. He had women hanging off him—

JUDITH: —but he chose me.

LYDIA: Excuse me, but that's my point: why on earth choose you?

HESTER: One of life's eternal mysteries.

JUDITH: I suppose I deserve this.

LYDIA: You *suppose?* You're the thing every wife dreads. You're disgusting!

JUDITH: I was the love of his life.

LYDIA: Crap.

JUDITH: It was incredibly special.

MERIDEE: Where did you go?

JUDITH: We went to New York, we went to Rome—

MERIDEE: I know you went to fucking Rome!

JUDITH: London, Paris, Madrid, Venezuela—

LYDIA: That's a bit off the beaten track for an affair, isn't it?.

JUDITH: We had fun together. It was like I was a completely different person—in a different world—in a different life—

MERIDEE: Alec never had fun, except when he was working.

HESTER: Perhaps he was just making sure *you* didn't have any.

JUDITH: We'd eat and eat and somehow I'd always come home ten pounds lighter.

HESTER: The pituitary gland getting an unaccustomed workout.

LYDIA: I don't believe this. I just don't believe it. Ten years!

MERIDEE: There are children who punish us for being their parents; perhaps there are spouses who punish us for having married them.

JUDITH: You weren't being punished. You didn't know. I couldn't bring myself to tell you. I waited for Alec to say something. I waited and waited. Finally I thought, he's never going to do it, so I asked him: 'When are you going to tell Meridee so we can be together?' and he said, 'That's your job'.

MERIDEE: What?

JUDITH: He wouldn't tell you himself, he expected me to.

LYDIA: What kind of a man is that?

HESTER: A coward.

LYDIA: Oh, come on. It means he wasn't in a tearing hurry to change his lifestyle.

JUDITH: But he didn't mind if *I* told. He said it was up to me.

HESTER: Perhaps in his mind you were interchangeable—sorry, Meridee.

JUDITH: [*to* MERIDEE] I couldn't tell you. You were my friend. I didn't want to hurt you.

LYDIA: Are you for real?

JUDITH: I couldn't do it. Several times I almost did—before the abortion—but I couldn't. So we'd go back to our normal horrible lives without each other.

MERIDEE: Horrible?

JUDITH: He'd shrug and say, 'Never mind, Judith, we can't eat cake all the time'.

MERIDEE: You were cake? What was I? Meat and potatoes?

JUDITH: You were the everyday.

MERIDEE: You were happy to be cake?

JUDITH: No, I wasn't happy to be cake. I wanted to be meat and potatoes too. We never even wrote letters. We just waited.

MERIDEE: For what?

LYDIA: All those guesthouses and weekend cottages in the Mountains.

JUDITH: Alec had a rule: we never made love in the same country Meridee was in.

LYDIA: Or the same country twice, from the sound of it.

HESTER: I know that rule. Some men interpret it as 'in the same city'. Country is limiting your field of activity quite markedly.

MERIDEE: Ten years…?

LYDIA: [*awed*] Alec wasn't your 'Mr Five Years Ago'—? No, of course not.

JUDITH: It ended before that.

MERIDEE: Why?

JUDITH: Because I had principles.

LYDIA: Hah!

JUDITH: I went on not being able to say anything and finally he just seemed to get bored. He said, 'Right, that's it'. [*To* MERIDEE] I'd been given the conditions: tell you myself or else.

MERIDEE: There must have been a reason. Alec always had a reason.

JUDITH: I read about him giving a paper in Stockholm. I hadn't even known he was overseas!

She is crying. Except for HESTER, *they are all increasingly 'tired and emotional'.*

I was lucky if I saw him once a year! What did I take from you? You took from me! Why didn't you leave?

MERIDEE: He was my husband! Why the hell should I?

JUDITH: You weren't happy!

MERIDEE: Compared with you we were bloody marvellous. Agonising over men... and Lydia and Gotme fighting all the time—

LYDIA: Thanks a bunch.

JUDITH: I kept waiting... wondering. But you know what I realised, Meridee? You were never going to leave. You were hooked on being the great man's wife. It's a big world out there, and you weren't exactly the life of the party. You didn't have the guts to make it alone. I did. I had the *guts!*

HESTER: Alec could have left and he didn't. Now why was that?

MERIDEE: Why would he—?

LYDIA: Couldn't live on cake.

MERIDEE: Who typed his manuscripts? Who organised his schedule? Who answered the phone, booked his tickets—

JUDITH: You were a secretary not a wife!

MERIDEE: —washed his dirty underwear, listened to his late-night ravings about multi-processor architectures, and the fact that he got his feet wet coming from the car and it was all my fault for stopping in the wrong place and he didn't have time to have a cold because his mind was on speeding up the fucking compiler! Who took him to the doctor, the dentist, the *airport* because he didn't drive? Who innocently came to meet him? How did you manage it, Judith—? I never caught sight of you once. You were peripheral.

JUDITH: [*getting up*] I'm not going to listen to this—

MERIDEE: [*pushing her down again*] Yes you are. Maybe you put yourself on hold waiting for your frequent-flyer fucks, but I put my entire life at the back of the wardrobe. A woman who lives with a man loses more than her own space, she loses time. Her *own time!* Alec kept saying soon it would be my turn. It was never my turn. Until the day he died there were students and colleagues here with notebooks and tape-recorders and video cameras, even when he was talking complete rubbish and had no idea who they were. He kept telling them to take out the garbage. He was fixated with garbage. Kept telling them it was piling up, which it was, mentally; it was all turning to garbage in his head. Garbage and *'Conchiglie Ulpia'*. I thought: if he thinks I'm Judith I'll behave like Judith—I couldn't see you wiping up his mess. I got less and less tolerant of him in really mean, nasty, petty ways. I kept telling myself: this is the Judith factor. It was payback time for all the things he'd done to me. I fell into a moral void, and fell, and fell. I got to a point where I loathed myself. I looked at him doddering and shitting and I thought: you're not going gently into that good night, you're not going to rage either; you're going to go shambling into the grave with me mopping up after you. But I couldn't walk out and leave him wallowing in his own excrement. And if I did, what would I live on? Claim support from a helpless invalid I'd abandoned?

She pours herself more whisky.

He was pointing at something, a bird or something, below the escarpment, and he turned and said, 'Look, darling'. He'd never called me darling in his life, so presumably it was aimed at you. Or some other woman—who knows? He said, 'Look, darling'. And I said, 'Yes, look', and I pushed him.

HESTER: What?

JUDITH: Jesus.

LYDIA: You really did it.

JUDITH: You pushed him over a cliff.

MERIDEE: He didn't spend his last days with me, he spent them with you.

JUDITH: You killed him!

LYDIA: Forget lemurs.

JUDITH: How can you sleep?

MERIDEE: I can't.

JUDITH: I'm going to the police.

MERIDEE: Go. I don't care anymore.

JUDITH: Did you ever care?

She grabs her bag. HESTER *bars the way.*

HESTER: Sit down.

JUDITH: Get out of my way.

She tries to push past. HESTER *stands firm.*

LYDIA: For God's sake, Judith, show some sense for once in your life. Think before you do something.

JUDITH: I don't need to think—

HESTER: And look where that approach has got you.

LYDIA: If you go to the police, what happens to us?

JUDITH: I don't care what happens to us.

LYDIA: 'The Secret Life of Alec Hobbes and his Women'? Do you want that plastered all over the tabloids and the TV? Great PR, Judith. Think how sticky your hands'd be then.

JUDITH: I owe it to Alec.

LYDIA: Owe what to Alec?

With surprising strength she bundles JUDITH *across the room and into a chair.*

Have a piece of chicken. [*She picks up a drumstick.*] Look. Chicken. Eat.

She shoves it into JUDITH*'s hand.*

JUDITH: Are you all nuts?

LYDIA: I can see them at the Leura Village Association. I'd have to leave the Mountains.

JUDITH: [*to* MERIDEE] I could *never* have done what you did. Never.

MERIDEE: I wonder.

JUDITH: [*to* LYDIA] I don't want this. Why are you giving me chicken?

She throws it on the floor.

MERIDEE: You never put yourself in my shoes, Judith.

JUDITH: I'm not my sister's keeper.

MERIDEE: No.

LYDIA: Age abuse! Roles get reversed when the abuser gets sick or old! I heard it on the car radio.

JUDITH: But you don't murder.

LYDIA: If all the men who betrayed their wives were pushed over cliffs, how many'd be left?

HESTER: [*delighted*] What a great little problem solver you are, Lydia!

LYDIA: Age abuse. What a fuckin' nightmare to look forward to.

JUDITH: Alec's dead! Doesn't anyone else care about that? If you know about it and you don't say anything, you're an accessory after the fact. We have to go to the police.

LYDIA: [*realising*] Otherwise we're all implicated—

MERIDEE: 'Each man's death diminishes me, for I am involved in mankind.'

JUDITH: I don't think she even knows what she's done.

LYDIA: [*hopefully*] Diminished responsibility?

JUDITH: We have to report it, Lydia. Now!

LYDIA: Gotme's been very nice to me lately...

JUDITH: I'm *talking* here—

MERIDEE: She's talking, Lydia.

LYDIA: Quite apart from the local scandal it would cause and the effect on business—Gotme is currently not being ungenerous, mostly because I currently hold the moral high ground.

JUDITH: What moral high ground?

LYDIA: He left me for a twenty-three-year-old!

She pours more whisky.

JUDITH: Don't have any more to drink, Lydia. We have to think clearly.

HESTER: That'll be a stretch.

JUDITH: Don't be so bloody patronising. Unlike you, I've been earning a living. I haven't had time to think.

HESTER: I agree that now would be a good time to start.

JUDITH: Moralising bitch, sponging your way in here. You make Rosie your problem and then you try and make her ours.

HESTER: She's not a problem! She's Rosie!

JUDITH: Farting around with women's issues and trees. Now you can't help a friend in trouble.

HESTER: She was your friend too.

JUDITH: She's got shelter, she's got food—

HESTER: She's killing herself!

JUDITH: If you'd had any foresight, you'd have a house by now and Rosie wouldn't be in this situation.

HESTER: You're saying it's my fault? Because I don't have a house?

JUDITH: Think about it, Hester.

HESTER: What's happened to you, Judith? You used to have a heart.

LYDIA: [*oblivious*] Twenty-three. A twenty-fuckin'-three-year-old. But at least I've got a thirty-year-old...

She reaches for her mobile and dials. JUDITH *descends abruptly into maudlin incoherence forgetting her intention to leave.*

JUDITH: He was a good man.

HESTER: [*hard*] Define good, Judith.

JUDITH: It's true! He wanted me to have his baby. He was a good, good man. I was worried about telling him, but he was delighted I was pregnant.

HESTER: Amazing.

JUDITH: [*annunciating carefully*] Not amazing, delighted.

HESTER: A Darwinian maximising his offspring.

JUDITH: He was a good, good man. He didn't want me to have an abortion.

MERIDEE: [*confused*] Which I seem to recall taking you to.

HESTER: You did take her. We discussed that.

JUDITH: You did take me, thank you very much, sweetheart. He was quite annoyed—

HESTER: Alec was not only stranger than we think, but stranger than we *can* think.

JUDITH: I couldn't do it to you, Meridee. I couldn't have his child—and here's the thanks I get: you kill him.

LYDIA: He's fucking not there…! I'll ring him at his friend's place… shit! I don't know the number!—

HESTER *is the only one remotely sober. She moves to the computer and stares at the screen.*

JUDITH: And what have I got now? Reading groups.

MERIDEE: Do you think George loved Charmian?

LYDIA: [*putting her mobile away*] Who?

JUDITH: George Johnston.

LYDIA: Loved who?

JUDITH: Charmian Clift.

MERIDEE: I don't think he loved her.

JUDITH: When she was young.

MERIDEE: Not when she was middle-aged.

JUDITH: Lot of passion when they were young.

MERIDEE: Cruel to her when they were middle-aged.

JUDITH: Put on weight and her teeth rotted.

MERIDEE: He had rotten teeth too.

JUDITH: But I think she still loved him.

LYDIA: Who're we talking about?

JUDITH: Wouldn't be any hoops without men.

LYDIA: Pass the bottle, Judith.

JUDITH *passes her the whisky.*

HESTER: [*still watching the computer screen*] Richard Dawkins would argue that a non-zero proportion of love was genetically provided for.

MERIDEE: Richard Dawkins is a happily… is happily married to that girl from *Dr Who*. He'd have to say that.

LYDIA: Richard who?

JUDITH: *Dr Who*.

LYDIA: I was happily married.

JUDITH: Bullshit.

LYDIA: For six months. Then I was unhappily married for twenty-four years and *three* months.

JUDITH: Did you love Gotme?

LYDIA: Must've. I torched his Ferrari.

HESTER *gets up from the computer.*

HESTER: [*thinking aloud*] Out of all the women in the world, including students, he picks his wife's best friend. Someone with a healthy income…

LYDIA: Gotme?

HESTER: Alec. Don't you find that interesting? He was delighted when Judith got pregnant, and annoyed when she didn't produce any offspring.

JUDITH: [*fuddled*] So?

MERIDEE: What're you saying?

HESTER: Any Darwinian organism has two main strategies for getting its genes into posterity: have lots of offspring, don't provide resources, and hope some survive—

MERIDEE: Or have fewer offspring…

HESTER: —and make sure they have a good chance of growing up. Alec knew Judith would look after it, whether he was in a long term relationship with her or not.

LYDIA: You saved yourself a bloody fortune, Judith, believe me.

HESTER: He may have been a genius, but anyone who thought artificial life forms were an adequate model for human behaviour wasn't exactly up there in the empathy stakes.

JUDITH: I don't get it—

HESTER: Having the two of you fight it out so he could enjoy the winner and start looking for another competitor as soon as possible?

JUDITH: Like who?

HESTER: A replacement extra-marital amenity.

JUDITH: You make me sound like a bloody toilet block! He *used* me?

LYDIA: Obviously he *used* you, you cluck—

HESTER: Both of you. [JUDITH *and* MERIDEE] You always need a variable.

JUDITH: He was experimenting with us?

HESTER: Not really. Let's give him the benefit of his moral indifference. Being able to program his life the way he wanted, it was simply a habit of mind—the way he manipulated the world and the people around him. He didn't get what he wanted from Judith though, did he?

MERIDEE: The ten-year toilet block amenity? I'd say he got a fair crack.

HESTER: In the end she did what really mattered: she put herself in someone else's shoes.

MERIDEE: In the end.

HESTER: Not everything in life is competition. Judith never wanted to hurt you.

MERIDEE: You didn't live the last few months as I lived them.

HESTER: None of us can imagine what that must have been like.

MERIDEE: I watched him fall. For a moment I think he recognised me. He looked surprised, as if he was thinking: 'Oh, Meridee, it's you after all'. And I wanted him back. I wanted that recognition.

HESTER: Which he never really gave you.

MERIDEE: Why do I feel as if I don't exist?

HESTER: Your most delicate feelings were ridiculed—spirit, soul, subtle connections between people and events. All the while being told you had no self and were no more valid than a life form in his computer.

MERIDEE: [*distressed*] He never said that.

HESTER: You typed his books.

MERIDEE: He never said it to me.

HESTER: He didn't need to. If you had to sum your life up in a single word, what would it be?

MERIDEE: I don't know. Don't ask me that. I don't know.

HESTER: A single word.

MERIDEE: Grief, I suppose. Grieving. But I don't know what for.

HESTER: Not being allowed to love?

MERIDEE: Not being allowed to love.

HESTER: I don't see a biological machine when I look at you; I see a woman in trouble. But I wonder what Alec saw?

MERIDEE: [*shaken*] I started thinking about his brain. It was like a program that had been corrupted. And I'd been deleted. If I wasn't part of the program, what was I?

HESTER: So you culled him.

MERIDEE *puts her head in her hands.*

It's what you did, Meridee. You culled him.

MERIDEE: [*in tears*] Please go away.

HESTER: He was a stupid man because he treated you badly.

MERIDEE: [*shaking her head*] Don't—

HESTER: You were following your best instincts, believing him and caring for him, even when instructed that there were no best instincts.

MERIDEE: Please, Hester.

HESTER: He lived by the meme, and he died by the meme. He invited his own death.

MERIDEE*'s defences are completely down.*

I don't want to hurt you.

MERIDEE: You are hurting me. Judith didn't hurt me. Not like you. Judith knew nothing. I'm not used to someone who understands.

LYDIA: Leave her alone, Hester.

HESTER *opens the stolen handbag and takes out the unknown woman's handkerchief. She gently dabs* MERIDEE*'s face.*

HESTER: Fortunately not everyone thinks like Alec. Yet.

JUDITH: [*not moving*] Maybe someone should make some coffee.

LYDIA: You know where the kitchen is.

JUDITH: I'm not leaving this room even for a pee.

MERIDEE: [*shaky*] I'm okay.

HESTER *puts the handkerchief back in the bag.*

Give it here and I'll wash it.

HESTER *gives it to her.* MERIDEE *blows her nose.*

LYDIA: How should we spend the rest of the weekend, girls? The Three Sisters? Scenic Railway? Vulcans?

HESTER: I'm off to Sydney.

JUDITH: Why? Haven't you had a good enough time moralising us to death?

HESTER: I'm heading back to Sydney, and then I'm going to the police.

There is a stunned moment while they take it in.

JUDITH: What did you say?

HESTER: It hasn't become legal yet to dispose of someone who's past their 'use by' date.

LYDIA: What are you talking about? I thought you were with us? I thought we were in this together?

HESTER: Not me, kiddos.

LYDIA: But we agreed!

HESTER: You agreed, I didn't.

JUDITH: [*confused*] *I* was the one going to the police, not you.

JUDITH, LYDIA *and* MERIDEE *rapidly become more focused.*

LYDIA: I thought we'd worked it out?

HESTER: You didn't ask me.

LYDIA: I *assumed—*

HESTER: Don't assume anything.

JUDITH: Not with you.

HESTER: Never with me.

LYDIA: Gotme will have a field day. I'll never hear the end of it. I'll be notorious.

JUDITH: We all will.

MERIDEE: [*with a shaky laugh*] And I'll be in jail.

LYDIA: I can't believe you'd do this.

HESTER: Despite all evidence to the contrary, I still think we live in a moral universe, not a moral vacuum. Call me sentimental if you like.

LYDIA: You were never sentimental.

JUDITH: We were friends—are friends. Doesn't friendship count?

HESTER: Depends how far it goes.

JUDITH: To the limit, surely?

HESTER: To the limit?

JUDITH: Absolutely.

LYDIA: It's like those miniseries about college friends who get together years later over some guilty secret—

JUDITH: What guilt? I don't feel guilty.

HESTER: Of course you do. The world wouldn't function if women didn't feel guilty about something. The thing is, though, I love Rosie, and I don't feel the least bit guilty over what I'm about to do.

LYDIA: What do you mean?

HESTER: Because you're going to pay.

LYDIA: For what?

HESTER: For Rosie. Open your bag.

LYDIA: What?

HESTER: You're not going deaf in your old age, are you? I thought it was just your memory. Give me your bag.

LYDIA: You've got this *thing* about bags—

JUDITH: I think she means it, Lydia.

LYDIA: *No way!*

JUDITH: You'd better give it to her.

LYDIA: Are you nuts?

JUDITH: Give her your fucking bag!

HESTER: Girls! Girls! Let's proceed in an orderly manner. There's a Mercedes outside with 'Free Tibet' on the back.

JUDITH: You're not serious?

HESTER: Oh, I'm serious.

JUDITH: It's blackmail!

HESTER: [*amused*] As against murder and accessories after the fact?

She holds out her hand for LYDIA*'s bag.*

LYDIA: [*snarling*] Don't even think about it.

HESTER: You haven't, obviously.

LYDIA: Think I'm stupid, don't you?

HESTER: No, I don't. I'm quite fond of you. Now give me your bag.

LYDIA: Will you take a cheque?

HESTER: No cheques.

LYDIA *hands over the bag.* HESTER *removes the jewellery. A keening sound comes from* LYDIA.

Car key, Judith.

JUDITH: No way. I didn't kill anyone.

HESTER: Didn't you? How much of Meridee's state of mind will be laid at your door, do you think?

JUDITH: [*shaken*] Who would think that?

HESTER: I do, for a start. Any good investigative journalist.

JUDITH: You're a monster.

HESTER: And you'll be infamous. It'll follow you the rest of your life.

JUDITH: I love that car. I paid for it in blood.

HESTER: [*not without sympathy*] Yes you did, apparently. But on your salary it shouldn't be too hard to replace it. Car key, Judith.
JUDITH: This is outrageous!
HESTER: So is the entire fucking social services system.
JUDITH: Oh. Well. If you put it that way.

She tosses the key to HESTER.

HESTER: Thank you.
JUDITH: You can't sell it without the registration papers anyway.
HESTER: Fine, then I'm a car-napper. You'll be getting a ransom note.
JUDITH: That car's my baby. Treat her with respect.
HESTER: What's it worth—ransom value?
JUDITH: Not enough for a house.

MERIDEE *picks up* HESTER*'s coat.*

I love that car.
LYDIA: I loved my rings.
JUDITH: She's got my jumper.
LYDIA: Stiff shit, Judith. I wish I had her working for me.

MERIDEE *holds out the coat.*

MERIDEE: Will you be okay driving?
JUDITH: It's very airtight—you can't fart in it without it hanging round. Good German engineering—

Suddenly the computer comes to life. The sound of a siren splits the air, followed by a nuclear explosion. JUDITH *screams. Instinctively the women duck for cover amidst the surround sound of bombs detonating. A helicopter gunship beats overhead, succeeded by a jaunty, cheeky little fanfare.* MERIDEE *turns off the speakers.*

LYDIA: What the fuck—?
MERIDEE: One of Alec's more cheerful little hobbies was to extrapolate upwards to the results of a real world war.
LYDIA: Oh, shit—

JUDITH *is collapsed on the floor.*

She's having a heart attack!
JUDITH: *I'm having a heart attack!*
HESTER: [*kneeling beside her*] Have you had a heart attack before, Judith?

JUDITH: People don't always know!

HESTER: Where's the pain?

JUDITH holds her head.

Your heart's in your head?

LYDIA: Figures.

JUDITH: I'm having a stroke like Rosemary! [*She looks up at* HESTER *fearfully.*] I'm going to be helpless and alone, in a room with horrible lighting and bad paintings—

MERIDEE *hands* HESTER *a glass of water.* HESTER *helps* JUDITH *drink.*

I'm scared, Hester.

HESTER: You're fine.

LYDIA: Get up, Judith.

JUDITH: I could be dying.

LYDIA: Afraid not.

She helps JUDITH *up.*

What the fuck happened?

The women are like shell-shocked survivors. With the exception of JUDITH *they gather around the computer screen staring at the critters.*

HESTER: [*reading off the screen*] 'Expected death of ninety-eight percent of intelligences and fifty-three percent of species. Destruction of resources, seventy-eight percent. Expected biome recovery time, one hundred and five years and ten months…'

MERIDEE: When a dot disappears, that's a colony. If a whole area goes dark, it's the end of a species.

LYDIA: This whole corner's gone.

JUDITH: The critters are killing each other?

MERIDEE: It's an extinction event. Some species won't return. They've had their chance and they haven't survived.

JUDITH: Those things aren't like us? It isn't real?

MERIDEE: What's real to you? Do you understand the billions of neurones, hormones and neuro-transmitters that make you want a plate of '*Conchiglie Ulpia*'—or someone else's husband?

LYDIA: You're saying she didn't know what she was doing?

MERIDEE: She knew what she was doing, but she didn't know why—any more than the critters know.

JUDITH: You're saying we're like them?

MERIDEE: No, because even if we don't understand what we do, we can think about the consequences. We can think about our values—

LYDIA: Ten years was a bloody long think!

MERIDEE: In the end we're not critters, we have choice. We're human beings.

HESTER: With extinction events.

JUDITH: [*to* MERIDEE] Did you think about your values when you pushed him?

MERIDEE: I behaved like one of his critters—blindly. As one can.

There is a silence. Impulsively LYDIA *removes her remaining rings. She turns to* HESTER.

LYDIA: Take these.

She hands HESTER *the rings.*

HESTER: [*surprised*] Thank you, Lydia. [*amused*] You don't have to strip yourself bare.

LYDIA: [*relieved*] Sure?

HESTER: [*returning the rings*] Keep them as a reminder.

LYDIA: [*replacing them*] Get a good price for the others. Don't let them go for a song. And don't try and sell them locally.

HESTER: I'm not stupid, Lydia.

LYDIA: Rosie's lucky to have you.

JUDITH: I notice you haven't asked Meridee to cough up.

MERIDEE: You'll let me know if there's anything I can do, won't you?

HESTER: I'm coming to Meridee.

LYDIA *takes out her mobile and dials.* HESTER *tosses the key. She seems to be waiting for something.*

LYDIA: Ah, fuck it! You're there or you're not there.

She stuffs the phone back in her bag. JUDITH *has been watching* HESTER.

JUDITH: It's still extortion. There are ways of doing things. It's my car.

LYDIA: It was your car.

JUDITH: Mine to give. You can't marginalise me. I won't be coerced.

She scribbles on a scrap of paper and hands it to HESTER.

This is my number. If you get pulled over, refer them to me. Say I loaned you the car for—for humanitarian reasons.

HESTER *envelops her in a hug.*

HESTER: You're going to be okay, Judith.

JUDITH: Am I?

HESTER: You are. You and Lydia: you're going to be fine.

JUDITH: Say hello to Rosemary from me. If she remembers.

HESTER: She remembers.

LYDIA: And me.

HESTER: You'd better give me your card.

LYDIA: What?

HESTER: Your business card. We'll come and visit you.

LYDIA: [*dismayed*] Me?

HESTER: Rosie'd like to see you when we move up here.

LYDIA: Remember what I said: it's not exactly cheap here anymore.

HESTER: We'll manage.

She takes LYDIA*'s card.*

LYDIA: To be strictly honest, you're going to need more than a house. You're going to need a proper income. Who's going to look after Rosie while you're swabbing toilet bowls? A car and my jewellery won't cut it.

HESTER: I'm aware of that.

LYDIA: Just so you know what you're getting yourself into.

JUDITH: You're a piece of work, Hester. You really are.

HESTER: Thank you.

JUDITH: You can give me back my jumper.

HESTER: I've put off the hair shirt, girls. [*Stroking the jumper*] I'm wearing cashmere from now on. Feels good too. Besides, it's not easy to give things back—you should ask Meridee. Sometimes it's impossible.

LYDIA: What do you mean?

HESTER: [*to* MERIDEE] Tell them about the days when Alec and I were colleagues.

LYDIA: When were you and Alec colleagues?

JUDITH: Oh, get your act together, Lydia!

HESTER: [*to* MERIDEE] You used to come and pick us up late at night from uni when we'd been working on the computer.

MERIDEE: Alec didn't drive. What's your point?

HESTER: We'd continue our discussions in the car. You were fascinated. You even chimed in. You understood enough to contribute. You understood when I told him he didn't know how he walked across a room, so how could he tell a computer how it's done if he didn't know how his own brain was doing it? I explained the advantages of doing it my way: that if you're evolving programs to do something, you don't need to know how they work. They find their own solutions—bottom up, not top down.

I went to Tassie that year. I came back after the break and discovered Alec had taken my algorithm, run it under his account for weeks of computing time, and published the results.

It was delightful after that: he was head of the department, passing comments on my hair, my clothes, and generally making my life a misery, constantly referring to me as 'that upstart feminist'. I was 'difficult to work with', 'emotional'. It was enough, in those days, to discredit every word I said.

JUDITH: Are you telling us frizzy hair and a boiler suit denied you a place in history?

HESTER: Alec denied me. He was first in the field, and *he* set the agenda for what would be explored. No one shared ideas with me anymore. People found they had other things to do. Suddenly there was nothing for *me* to do. No reason to be in there every day. No reason to be alive.

She looks at MERIDEE.

[*Calmly*] I remember driving over to your place in that old Vee-Dub that was always breaking down, knowing Alec wasn't home, and as I came up the drive I was crying and I hit one of those garden lights. You heard the smash and you came out. I remember the look of concern on your face. I thought: it's going to be okay. Meridee understands bottom up from top down. I got out of the car and you said, 'Is everything all right—?'

I said, 'No, it's not all right'. And I told you how you could make it all right, how you could get me re-instated with my work properly acknowledged.

And what did you say, Meridee?

MERIDEE: He was my husband.

HESTER: And I was your friend. You knew what he owed me.

MERIDEE: What was I supposed to say? What could I have done?

HESTER: Told the truth.

MERIDEE: Who would have believed me anyway?

HESTER: You didn't even try to find out. Alec never looked back after that. And neither did you.

MERIDEE: You've no idea what you put me through, Hester.

HESTER: What I put you through?

MERIDEE: I had a six-month-old baby. What was I supposed to do? Destroy my husband's career?

LYDIA: That's a big ask.

JUDITH: Very big.

LYDIA: Did you try putting yourself in Meridee's shoes?

MERIDEE: It would be nice to think that in a crisis we're all going to behave well, but we don't. Unlike you, I wasn't resourceful, I wasn't bold, I wasn't clever—

LYDIA: I think murder's pretty bold.

MERIDEE: I'm sorry if you've held a grudge against me all these years—

HESTER: I never held a grudge. When I thought about you at all, I felt sorry for you.

MERIDEE: Sorry for me?

HESTER: Then Rosie got ill. Then Alec died. I'm not here for cars or jewellery—

LYDIA: Thank god for that.

MERIDEE: What do you want, Hester?

HESTER: First thing Monday you'll go to a lawyer and have all of Alec's intellectual property made over to me.

MERIDEE: What?

HESTER: You heard me.

MERIDEE: I can't do that.

HESTER: You certainly can.

MERIDEE: They'll think I'm of unsound mind!

HESTER: You'll have two partially sane witnesses to attest to your sanity. And you'll have a house free of Alec. You won't be haunted any more.

MERIDEE: You're taking the computer.

HESTER: As soon as the first royalty cheque arrives and I have somewhere for you to send it. I suspect it's going to make me eminently employable again.

MERIDEE: It's Alec's life's work.

HESTER: It should have been mine. Put yourself in my shoes, Meridee: extinction events happening on the hour, time running out for me to do anything useful—hickory dickory dock.

MERIDEE: What will you do with it?

HESTER: Add something Alec left out, and watch the critters evolve differently.

MERIDEE: Add what?

HESTER: I don't know yet—that's the fun part. Wishful thinking, but subtlety might be a good start—something that might lead to longer-term thinking. A strategy for human survival? Who knows? In the meantime—

She picks up her dero coat.

MERIDEE: In the meantime what …?

HESTER: I'll be going. [*Putting her coat on*] No need to see me out.

JUDITH: Hang on a minute!

HESTER: Watch out for each other. Take care.

She turns to leave.

LYDIA: What about my rings?

JUDITH: My car!

LYDIA: You don't need them now!

HESTER: Don't I?

LYDIA: That computer stuff's worth more than the house and land together!

HESTER: Talk to Meridee.

She moves to exit.

LYDIA: Meridee? Why Meridee?

HESTER *turns.*

HESTER: Haven't I taught you anything about blackmail? It's up to her when, or if, you get them back.

JUDITH *and* LYDIA *take this in.*

Enjoy the weekend, girls. Have fun.

She exits.

JUDITH *and* LYDIA *stare at* MERIDEE *as the lights fade.*

THE END

GRIFFIN THEATRE COMPANY PRESENTS

GRIFFIN
THEATRE
COMPANY

WICKED SISTERS

REGINALD THEATRE,
SEYMOUR CENTRE
6 NOVEMBER – 12 DECEMBER

BY ALMA DE GROEN

DIRECTOR
NADIA TASS

DESIGNER
TOBHIYAH STONE FELLER

LIGHTING DESIGNER
TRENT SUIDGEEST

COMPOSER & SOUND DESIGNER, VIDEO DESIGNER
NATE EDMONDSON

STAGE MANAGER
ISABELLA KERDIJK

WITH
DI ADAMS
VANESSA DOWNING
DEBORAH GALANOS
HANNAH WATERMAN

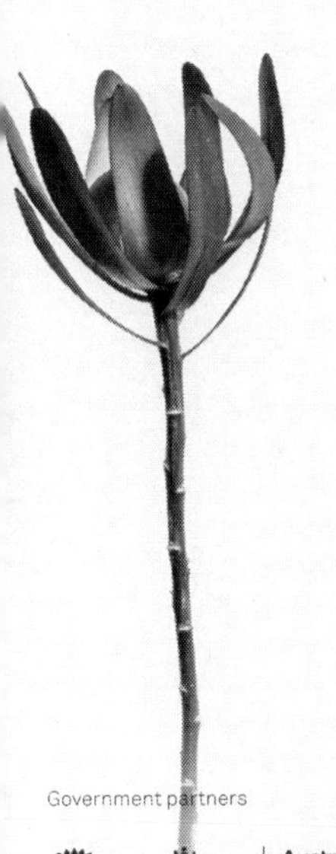

Government partners

Griffin acknowledges the generosity of the Seaborn, Broughton & Walford Foundation in allowing it the use of the SBW Stables Theatre rent free, less outgoings, since 1986.

PLAYWRIGHT'S NOTE

One day in the 1990s, outside the newsagent in Leura, I saw one of those yellow billboards with giant black lettering. In the 1980s they'd often been irresistible: 'DEAD HEART SOAKED!', or 'DRUNK ON MOON!' and I'd sometimes collect them. In the 1990s, this one featured Germaine Greer, so I went in the shop and asked if I could have it. "Who's Germaine Greer?", the young guy said. Perhaps I shouldn't have been shocked. Second Wave feminists were fading, and it was disturbing to learn that many of these dedicated lives were ending in poverty. This set me thinking about the fate of women in general, and how vulnerable some of us are as we age. We didn't see these women on stage then, or not often, and hardly ever centre stage, with all their gallantry and insecurities. I, for one, wanted to see them. But it turned out few of the people in charge agreed. The play was accepted for workshopping at the Australian National Playwrights' Centre, but only one theatre was willing to program it. And, after a long and respected history, that theatre announced it would close. That seemed to be it for *Wicked Sisters*—until Ros Horin and Playworks gave it a workshop (and Ros gave the play its name)—and in 2002, Griffin took it on. It did well, and went on to tour Victoria, Tasmania, Queensland and the Northern Territory—then it largely sank back into suspended animation in Australia, until Lee Lewis decided to revive it here.

The other thing I'd had a yen to see in those days was women on stage getting a chance to give voice to ideas, entertainingly and with relish. I'd been admiring of Eva Cox and her 1995 Boyer Lectures, 'A Truly Civil Society'. Having around that time written a play, *The Woman in the Window*, about a society in Australia's future that was anything but civil, I remained concerned about how we behave towards one another and the way in which current (1990s) thinking might shape our futures. *Wicked Sisters* remains as it was when written at the end of last century. I've made no attempt to update the science or technology, thus it's possible to assess how things have played out.

Interestingly enough, it has found an audience lately in Eastern Europe.

Alma De Groen
Playwright

DIRECTOR'S NOTE

Wicked Sisters focuses on the relationships of four divergent women. I am fascinated with their friendships and the slow revelation of rifts, deceptions and betrayals. My wish is that *Wicked Sisters* will inspire and empower women and men to confront the truth; for women to challenge those women whose friendships cannot be trusted; for women to oppose the men who would deny them their very own endeavours; and finally, to move away from being the victims and to become proactive in liberating themselves from self-deception and abuse.

The play is ostensibly about women's relationships—in this case with the same man who was a misogynist and brutally selfish, but a genius whose contribution to science was prodigious.

In a broader sense, the play looks at our future, at the tenuous balance of emotional, social and rational intelligence that will play out in our ultimate survival.

It also explores the moral and ethical codes that are broken, of four women struggling to re-find their self-esteem as the loss of *le grand savant* becomes a reality and unravels their world and their security.

Wicked Sisters is an absorbing narrative, full of tension and personal ambition. It is at this meeting of the four women that we unpack and discover the drive behind each one's betrayal. And we drill deep into their individual relationships with Alec, the man, who is ever-present, but who is not at this meeting.

Nadia Tass
Director

ALMA DE GROEN

PLAYWRIGHT

Alma De Groen was born in New Zealand in 1941. At the age of twenty-three she settled in Australia where, under the influence of the new theatre movement, she began writing plays in 1968. Her plays have been developed and produced all over the world, and include: for Nimrod Theatre Company: *The Sweatproof Boy*; for Grant Street Theatre: *Chidley*; for Jane Street Theatre: *The After-Life of Arthur Cravan*; for Melbourne Theatre Company: *Going Home*, *Vocations*, *The Woman in the Window* (which was shortlisted for the NSW Premier's Literary Awards); for Russell Street Theatre: *The Girl Who Saw Everything*, for which she was awarded the 1993 AWGIE Award for Best Stage Play; for Sydney Theatre Company: *The Rivers of China*, which won the Premier's Literary Award for Drama in both New South Wales and Victoria; and internationally: for The Drama Theatre of Ho Chi Minh City (Vietnam): *The Girl Who Saw Everything*; for the Studio Laboratory Theatre (Toronto, Canada): *The Joss Adams Show*. Alma was also Co-Writer and Dramaturg for Legs on the Wall's 1994 performance piece *Wildheart*. Alma's television credits include: for ABC: *After Marcuse*, *Man of Letters*, for which she was awarded the 1985 AWGIE Award; for Seven Network: *Rafferty's Rules*, *Singles*; and her work for radio includes *Available Light* and *Stories in the Dark* (with Ian MacKenzie), which was the Australian entry for the Prix Italia in 1996. In November 1998, Alma was the first playwright to win the Patrick White Literary Award for her contribution to Australian theatre. Alma's play *Wicked Sisters* was workshopped at the Australian National Playwrights' Conference 2001, and was produced by Griffin Theatre Company (under the direction of Kate Gaul) in 2002. It has enjoyed a season in Poland and the Czech Republic and has been translated for performance in France, along with *The Rivers of China*. Alma is currently retired in New Zealand, with her plays still being performed both in Australia and around the world.

NADIA TASS

DIRECTOR

Awarded the Screen Leader Award for Outstanding Leadership, Nadia Tass is one of Australia's most iconoclastic directors of both stage and screen. Nadia's experience as theatre director is extensive and diverse, ranging from improvised, classic, to contemporary and musical theatre. In recent years, theatre credits include: for Ensemble Theatre: *e-baby*, *Sorting Out Rachel*; for Melbourne Theatre Company: *Così*, *Miss Bosnia*, *The Other Place*, *Summer of the Aliens*; for Melbourne Theatre Company/Queensland Theatre/Geelong Performing Arts Centre: *Disgraced*; for The Production Company: *Promises, Promises*; for Red Stitch Actors Theatre: *The Aliens*, *Extinction*, *The Gronholm Method*, *Out of the Water*, *Uncle Vanya*; for Red Stitch Actors Theatre/Queensland Theatre: *The Flick*; for Sport for Jove: *Ear to the Edge of Time*; for Victorian Arts Centre/Malcolm C Cooke and Associates Pty Ltd.: *The Lion, the Witch and the Wardrobe*, which garnered a nomination for Best Director of a Musical at the Helpmann Awards; and internationally: for 59E59 Theaters/New Jersey Repertory Company (US): *Fern Hill*; for King's Head Theatre (UK): *Three Women in an Ice Cream Cone*; for King's Head Theatre (UK)/Southbank Theatre (AU): *The Book Club*; for Portland Stage (US): *Sex and Other Disturbances*; and for Signature Theatre (US): *Masterpieces*. Nadia is a multi-award winning film director. Her films include *Amy*, *The Big Steal*, *Fatal Honeymoon*, *Malcolm*, *Matching Jack*, *Mr Reliable*, *Pure Luck*, *Rikky and Pete,* and on television, the mini-series *Stark* for the BBC. She directs films for major studios and networks in America, including A&E Network, CBS, Disney, Universal Studios, and Warner Bros. In 2012, Nadia was honoured by the American Cinematheque with a retrospective of her film work in Los Angeles.

TOBHIYAH STONE FELLER

DESIGNER

Tobhiyah is a multi-disciplinary designer dedicated to live performance, interior, and installation projects. Based in Sydney, Tobhi is also a Lecturer in the Design and Creative Practice Centres at NIDA, where she graduated in 2005. Set & Costume Design credits include: for Griffin: *Replay*, *Splinter*; for Griffin Independent: *Lighten Up*; for ATYP: *Bustown*, *Desiree Din and the Red Forest*, *The Laramie Project*, *This Territory*; for B Sharp: *A View of Concrete*; for Bell Shakespeare Education: *Macbeth*; for Blacktown Arts Centre: *My Name is SUD*; for Clockfire Theatre Co/ Sydney Festival: *Night Parade of One Hundred Goblins*; for Ensemble: *Blue/Orange*, *Clybourne Park*, *e-baby*, *Good People*, *My Zinc Bed/Blood Bank*, for which her multi-purpose set design won the Installation Design Category at the 2016 Australian Interior Design Awards, *Sorting Out Rachel*; for Merrigong Theatre Company: *Camarilla*; for Musica Viva: *Da Vinci's Apprentice*; *Hercules*; for Performing Lines: *Variant*; for Riverside Theatres: *Parramatta Girls*; for Siren Theatre Company: *Human Resources*; for Sydney Conservatorium of Music: *Daisy Bates at Ooldea*, *Orphée Aux Enfers*; and for Tamarama Rock Surfers: *Anna Robi and the House of Dogs*. In 2014, Tobhiyah was awarded Highly Commended Emerging Designer for Stage at the Australian Production Design Guild Awards. In 2019, *Flowstate*, a multi-arts outdoor performance venue for which she was a lead designer was awarded The Great Place Award by QLD Planning Institute of Australia. Tobhiyah is an active member of Australian Production Design Guild for which she is the Live Performance Coordinator of the MENTORAPDG program.

TRENT SUIDGEEST
LIGHTING DESIGNER

Trent Suidgeest's lighting design credits include: for Griffin: *First Love is the Revolution*, *Prima Facie*, *The Feather in the Web*, *Kill Climate Deniers*, *The Homosexuals or 'Faggots'*; for Belvoir/Black Swan State Theatre Company: *The Sapphires* (which toured to the Barbican Centre, London and Daegu Opera House, South Korea); for Black Swan State Theatre Company: over 20 mainstage productions, recently including *Oklahoma!*, *Summer of the Seventeenth Doll*; for Black Swan State Theatre Company/Melbourne Theatre Company: *National Interest*; for Darlinghurst Theatre Company: *The Rise and Fall of Little Voice*; for Ensemble Theatre: *Black Cockatoo*, *Folk*; for Global Creatures: *Muriel's Wedding The Musical* (also at Sydney Theatre Company), for Hayes Theatre Company: *Calamity Jane* (including Australian Tour and Belvoir), *Darlinghurst Nights*, *Gypsy*, *Merrily We Roll Along*, *Only Heaven Knows*, *The Rise and Disguise of Elizabeth R*, *The View UpStairs*; for Opera Australia: *Carmen*, *Sydney Opera House—The Opera (The Eighth Wonder)*, *The Rabbits*; for The Production Company: *The Boy From Oz*, *Dusty*, *Jesus Christ Superstar*, *The King & I*, *Nice Work If You Can Get It*; for Red Line Productions: *Betty Blokk-Buster Reimagined;* for Sydney Theatre Company: *Accidental Death of an Anarchist*, *Hay Fever*, *Talk.* In 2015, with a Mike Walsh Fellowship, Trent assisted Jan Versweyveld and Ivo van Hove at Toneelgroep Amsterdam on their Shakespearian epic *Kings of War* at Wiener Festwochen.

NATE EDMONDSON
COMPOSER & SOUND DESIGNER, VIDEO DESIGNER

Nate is an international, multi-award-winning composer and sound designer for stage and screen. His theatre credits include: for Griffin: *Caress/Ache*, *Dead Cat Bounce*, *Good Cook. Friendly. Clean.*, *Jump for Jordan*, *This Year's Ashes*, *The Witches*; for Griffin Independent: *The Ham Funeral*, *Rust and Bone*, *MinusOneSister*, *Music*; for ATYP: *Fireface*, *The Hiding Place*, *Political Children*; for Bell Shakespeare: *A Midsummer Night's Dream*, *Julius Caesar*, *Macbeth*, *Romeo and Juliet*, *The Tempest*, *The Winter's Tale*; for Belvoir: *Mark Colvin's Kidney*, *Mortido*, *Seventeen*, *This Heaven*; for Critical Stages: *Stones in His Pockets*; for Darlinghurst Theatre Company: *All My Sons*, *Daylight Saving*, *Good Works*, *Love*, *Savages*, *The Seafarer*, *The Paris Letter*, *Torch Song Trilogy*; for Ensemble Theatre: *Baby Doll*, *Diplomacy*, *Fully Committed*; for Hayes Theatre Company: *Evie May*, *H.M.S. Pinafore*; for KXT:

Coram Boy, *Jatinga*, *Leaves*, for which Nate won the 2016 Broadway World Award for Best Score/Sound Design of a Play; for Little Ones Theatre: *Psycho Beach Party*, *Salomé*, *Two by Two*; for Malthouse Theatre: *Lord of the Flies*, *Salomé*; for Monkey Baa: *Edward The Emu*, *Possum Magic*; for New Theatre: *Marat/Sade*, *When The Rain Stops Falling*; for Red Line Productions at the Old Fitz: *Anatomy Of A Suicide*, *Bengal Tiger at the Baghdad Zoo*, *I Am My Own Wife*, *Our Blood Runs in the Street*, *The Village Bike*; for Riverside Theatres: *Shellshock*; for Rockefeller Productions: *Paddington Gets In A Jam* (US), *That Golden Girls Show!* (US & CA), *The Very Hungry Caterpillar Show* (AU, NZ, US, UAE, EU & UK); for Seymour Centre: *Blackrock*, *The Flick*, *Table*; for Siren Theatre Company: *Good With Maps* (AU & UK), *Misterman* (AU & UK), for both of which Nate won the Sydney Theatre Award for Best Score/Sound Design of an Independent Production, *The Moors*, *The Trouble With Harry*; for Sport For Jove: *Of Mice and Men*; for Street Theatre: *All My Sons* (UK), for which Nate won the 2014 Brian Dyer Trophy for Best Score/Sound Design; for Sydney Dance Company: *Once We Were*; for Sydney Theatre Company: *A Midsummer Night's Dream*, *Blackie Blackie Brown*, *Cloud Nine*, *The Harp in the South Parts I and II*, for which Nate was nominated for the Helpmann Award for Best Sound Design, *Never Did Me Any Harm* (with Force Majeure), *Romeo and Juliet*, *Three Sisters*.

ISABELLA KERDIJK

STAGE MANAGER

Isabella graduated from the production course at the National Institute of Dramatic Art in 2008. She has worked as stage manager and assistant stage manager on many shows, including: for Griffin: *And No More Shall We Part*, *Replay*, *The Smallest Hour*, *This Year's Ashes*, *Ugly Mugs*; for Belvoir: *An Enemy of the People*, *The Dog/The Cat*, *The Drover's Wife*, *Every Brilliant Thing*, *Fangirls*, *Girl Asleep*, *The Glass Menagerie*, *HIR*, *Jasper Jones*, *Kill the Messenger*, *Mother*, *Mother Courage and Her Children*, *My Name is Jimi*, *Stories I Want to Tell You In Person* (National Tour), *The Sugar House*, *Thyestes* (European Tours), *Winyanboga Yurringa*; for Circus Oz: *Cranked Up*; for Darlinghurst Theatre Company: *Fourplay*, *Ride*, *Silent Night*; for Ensemble Theatre: *Rainman*, *The Ruby Sunrise*; for Legs on the Wall: *Bubble*; for LWAA: *The Mousetrap* (Australia/New Zealand Tours); for Spiegelworld: *Empire*. Isabella has worked as Production Coordinator on *Carmen* (Opera Australia on Sydney Harbour) and Production Manager/Stage Manager for *Puppetry of the Penis* (A-List Entertainment). She has also worked on various festivals, including The Garden of Unearthly Delights, Sydney Festival and the Woodford Folk Festival.

DI ADAMS
HESTER

Di most recently appeared on stage in the 2020 production of *Australian Open* for Bub and the 2019 production of *Trevor* for Outhouse Theatre, both at KXT. Other stage credits include: for Apocalypse Theatre Company/Old 505: *All My Sleep and Waking*; for Bell Shakespeare: *King Lear*; for Ensemble Theatre: *When Dad Married Fury*; for MopHead Productions/Red Line Productions at the Old Fitz: *The Humans*; for New Theatre: *Parramatta Girls*; and for Sydney Theatre Company: *The Crucible*, *Tartuffe*. Di has worked extensively on screen, with her most recent film credits including: *All God's Creatures*, *Cherith*, *Help Me*, *Rust Bucket*, *The Turning*, *The War Room*, *The Water Diary*; and on television, credits include: for BBC UKTV: *Top of the Lake: China Girl*; for Foxtel: *Secret City*; for Network Ten: *Wake In Fright*; for SBS: *The Principal*; for Stan: *The Other Guy*. Di has also voiced numerous characters in children's television series: for ABC: *Sally Bollywood: Super Detective*; for Nine Network: *Seaside Hotel*; for Seven Network: *Raggs*; and for Stan: *Alice Miranda Friends Forever*. Di has been a proud member of Actors Equity since 1983.

VANESSA DOWNING
MERIDEE

Vanessa has enjoyed an extensive and varied career encompassing film, theatre and television. On stage, she has worked with many of Australia's leading theatre companies, of which highlights include: for Griffin: *Away*, *Live Acts on Stage*; for Griffin Independent: *Thomas Murray and the Upside Down River*; for Bell Shakespeare: *The Taming of the Shrew*; for Belvoir/Sydney Theatre Company/Sydney Festival: *A Cheery Soul*; for Ensemble Theatre: *The Glass Menagerie*; for The Production Company: *Hello, Dolly!*; for Queensland Theatre: *Season's Greetings*; for State Theatre Company South Australia: *As You Like It*, *Equus*, *Three Birds Alighting on a Field*, *Private Lives*, *Who's Afraid of Virginia Woolf?*; for Studio Co./Riverside Theatres: *King Lear*; for Sydney Theatre Company: *Black is the New White*, *The Deep Blue Sea*, *How to Rule the World*, *Macbeth*, *Power Plays*; and for Wilton Morley Productions: *Steaming*. On screen, Vanessa recently appeared in Season 2 of Foxtel's *Mr Inbetween*. Additional television credits include: for ABC: *Black Comedy*, *The Checkout*, *G.P.*, *Rake*; for Seven Network: *A Country Practice*, *All Saints*, *Home and Away*. Feature film appearances include: *The Boy Who Had Everything*, *Mary*, *Stationery*, *Two Hands*. Vanessa is also a member of the Sydney Philharmonia Symphony Chorus. Vanessa is a proud member of Actors Equity and is delighted to be returning to Griffin in *Wicked Sisters*.

DEBORAH GALANOS

LYDIA

Deborah is a graduate of the National Institute of Dramatic Art (NIDA), Trinity College London, the University of Sydney, and has worked all over Australia. Deborah's theatre credits include: for Griffin's Batch Festival/National Theatre of Parramatta/Sydney Festival: *Lady Tabouli*; for Apocalypse Theatre Company/Red Line Productions at the Old Fitz: *Metamorphoses*; for Bontom/Seymour Centre: *Unfinished Works*; for Bontom/Old 505: *Homesick*; for Belvoir: *Greek Tragedy*; for Burberry Productions: *Mum's the Word*; for Darlinghurst Theatre Company: *I'm With Her*, *The Mystery of Love & Sex*; for the Depot Theatre/Secret House: *The Seagull*; for Ensemble Theatre: *The God Committee*, *The Heartbreak Kid*; for The Goods Theatre Company/Red Line Productions at the Old Fitz: *Dropped*; for Mantouridion Theatre: *The Plot*; for MopHead Productions/Red Line Productions at the Old Fitz: *The House of Ramon Iglesia*; for NIDA Company: *Hotel Hibiscus*; for Sport for Jove: *Antigone, Romeo & Juliet*; for State Theatre Company South Australia: *Gods of Strangers*; for Sydney Festival: *Boswell for the Defence*; for Sydney Theatre Company/Australian People's Theatre: *The Shearston Shift*; and for theatrongroup: *Who's Afraid of Virginia Woolf?*. Deborah's television credits include: for ABC: *Children's Hospital*, *My Place*, *Police Rescue*, *Pulse*, *Rake*, *Redfern Now*; for NBC: *Camp*; for Network Ten: *Street Smart*; for Nine Network: *Murder Call*; and for Seven Network: *A Country Practice*, *All Saints*, *G.P.*, *Home and Away*. Her film credits include *Balls*, *Boys from the Bush*, *Cavity*, *Chasing Comets*, *Inside Out*, *No Worries*, *The Premonition*, and *Razzle Dazzle*. Deborah has been nominated for several Sydney Theatre Awards, and has been a proud Actors Equity Member since 1990.

HANNAH WATERMAN

JUDITH

Hannah began her career with the National Youth Theatre of Great Britain and went on to star in a wide variety of British television shows and stage productions. Hannah has toured the UK and appeared on the West End with a variety of shows including: for Anvil Arts: *Calendar Girls* (Tour and West End); *Tom, Dick and Harry* (West End); *Strangers on a Train* (Tour), *Vagina Monologues* (London and Tour); for Stephen Joseph Theatre: *Soap*; and *Abigail's Party* (Tour). Hannah's Australian theatre credits include: for Griffin: *The Almighty Sometimes*; for CDP Theatre Producers at Sydney Opera House: *Mr Stink*; for Christine Harris and HIT Productions: *Love Letters* (Tour); for Ensemble Theatre: *The Kitchen Sink*; for Hayes Theatre Company: *Side Show*; for Michael Cassell Group: *Harry Potter and the Cursed Child*; for Red Line Productions at the Old Fitz: *The Whale*; for Sydney Theatre Company: *Talk*. Hannah's film credits include *Patient 17*. Hannah's television credits include: for BBC: *Come Fly With Me*, *Dangerfield*, *Doctors*, *New Tricks*; for ITV: *Peak Practice*; and for London Weekend Television: *Tess of the D'Urbervilles*. In 2000, Hannah joined the cast of the British soap opera *EastEnders* (BBC) where she remained for four and a half years, appearing in over 400 episodes. Hannah is a proud member of Actors Equity and is thrilled to be back at Griffin!

ABOUT GRIFFIN

Griffin is the only theatre company in the country entirely devoted to producing new Australian plays. Located in the historic SBW Stables Theatre, nestled in the heart of bustling Kings Cross, Griffin has been a permanent home for the exploration of Australian stories since 1978.

Many of this country's most beloved and celebrated artists started out on our stage—Cate Blanchett, Michael Gow, Louis Nowra, David Wenham, to name a few—and iconic Australian plays like *The Boys*, *Holding the Man* and *The Bleeding Tree* had their world premieres at Griffin, before going on to capture the national imagination. We are a theatre of first chances.

We are passionate about nurturing emerging artists. We help ambitious, bold, risk-taking and urgent Australian plays get from a page onto a stage. We tell the stories that will help us know who we are as a nation, and who we want to become.

Stories about us. Written by us. For us.

At Griffin Theatre Company, we acknowledge that our home — the SBW Stables Theatre—is built on the unceded land of the Gadigal People of the Eora Nation. It is a privilege to perform on this land, which has been a place of story, song, and community for tens of thousands of years. We offer deep and humble respect to Gadigal elders, past and present. This always was, always will be Aboriginal land.

GRIFFIN THEATRE COMPANY
13 Craigend St
Kings Cross NSW 2011

02 9332 1052
info@griffintheatre.com.au
griffintheatre.com.au

SBW STABLES THEATRE
10 Nimrod St
Kings Cross NSW 2011

BOOKINGS
griffintheatre.com.au
02 9361 3817

GRIFFIN FAMILY

PATRON

Seaborn Broughton & Walford Foundation

Griffin acknowledges the generosity of the Seaborn, Broughton & Walford Foundation in allowing it the use of the SBW Stables Theatre rent free, less outgoings, since 1986.

BOARD

Bruce Meagher (Chair)
Simon Burke AO
Lyndell Droga
Tim Duggan
Declan Greene
Mario Philippou
Julia Pincus
Lenore Robertson
Simone Whetton
Meyne Wyatt

ARTISTIC

Artistic Director & CEO
Declan Greene

Associate Artistic Director
Tessa Leong

Artistic Associate
Phil Spencer

Literary Associates
Julian Larnach
Poppy Tidswell

ADMINISTRATION

Interim Executive Director and Head of Marketing
Fiona Hulton

Associate Producer - Development
Frankie Greene

Associate Producer - Programming
Imogen Gardam

Marketing Coordinator
AJ Lamarque

Communications Coordinator
Ang Collins

Development Coordinator
Ell Katte

Program & Administration Coordinator
Whitney Richards

Strategic Insights Consultant
Peter O'Connell

PRODUCTION

Production Manager
Ryan Garreffa

Production Coordinator
Ally Moon

FINANCE

Finance Consultant
Tracey Whitby

Finance Manager
Kylie Richards

CUSTOMER RELATIONS

Box Office Manager
Dominic Scarf

Bar Manager
Grace Nye-Butler

Customer Relations Team
Ell Katte
Julian Larnach
Poppy Tidswell

Sustainability Coordinators
Ang Collins
Grace Nye-Butler

BRAND AND GRAPHIC DESIGN
Alphabet Studio

COVER PHOTOGRAPHY
Brett Boardman

GRIFFIN DONORS

Income from Griffin activities covers less than 40% of our operating costs—leaving an ever increasing gap for us to fill through government funding, sponsorship and the generosity of our individual supporters. Your support helps us bridge the gap and keep ticket prices affordable and our work at its best. To make a donation and a difference, contact Griffin on **9332 1052** or donate online at **griffintheatre.com.au**

COMPANY PATRONS
Merilyn Sleigh
& Raoul de Ferranti

PRODUCTION PATRON
Girgensohn Foundation

PROGRAM PATRONS
Season Partner
Neilson Foundation

Griffin Ambassadors
Robertson Foundation

Griffin Studio Ensemble
Mary Ann Rolfe

Griffin Studio
Gil Appleton
Darin Cooper Foundation
Kiong Lee & Richard Funston
Rosemary Hannah &
Lynette Preston
Ken & Lilian Horler
Pip Rath & Wayne Lonergan
Malcolm Robertson Foundation
Mary Ann Rolfe
Geoff & Wendy Simpson
Danielle Smith
Walking up the Hill Foundation

Griffin Women's Initiative
Griffin Women's Initiative is supported by Creative Partnerships Australia through Plus1

Katrina Barter
Wendy Blacklock
Christy Boyce &
Madeleine Beaumont
Laura Crennan
Lyndell Droga
Melinda Graham
Sherry Gregory
Antonia Haralambis
Ann Johnson
Roanne Knox
Julia Pincus
Ruth Ritchie
Lenore Robertson
Sonia Simich
Margie Sullivan
Simone Whetton

SEASON PATRONS
As a new writing theatre, we program a wide range of stories that reflect our time, place and the unique voice of contemporary Australia. To ensure that these stories continue to be told, Griffin needs the help of private support to bring strength, insight, candour and new and powerful visions to the stage. Our Production Partner program is vital to our continued artistic success.

PRODUCTION PARTNERS 2020

Kindness by Matthew Whittet
Darin Cooper Foundation

PRODUCTION PARTNERS 2019

Prima Facie by Suzie Miller
Robert Dick & Erin Shiel
Richard McHugh
& Kate Morgan
Andrew Post & Sue Quill
Richard Weinstein
& Richard Benedict

City of Gold by Meyne Wyatt
Andrew Cameron AM & Cathy Cameron
Bruce Meagher & Greg Waters
Julia Pincus & Ian Learmonth
Malcolm Robertson Foundation
David Marr &
Sebastian Tesoriero
The Sky Foundation
Kim Williams AM &
Catherine Dovey
Ann & Brian O'Connell (in memoriam)

Splinter by Hilary Bell
Stephen Fitzgerald

SEASON DONORS
Front Row Donors
$10,000+
Andrew Cameron AM & Cathy Cameron
Darin Cooper Foundation
Robert Dick & Erin Shiel
Gordon & Marie Esden
Stephen Fitzgerald
Girgensohn Foundation
Rosemary Hannah &
Lynette Preston
Belinda Hazelton &
Vicki Archer
Ingrid Kaiser
Malcolm Robertson
Foundation
Sophie McCarthy &
Antony Green
Richard McHugh &
Kate Morgan
Bruce Meagher & Greg Waters
Neilson Foundation
Peter & Dianne O'Connell
Rebel Penfold-Russell OAM
Julia Pincus & Ian Learmonth
Pip Rath & Wayne Lonergan
Robertson Foundation
Mary Ann Rolfe
Ruth Ritchie
The Sky Foundation

GRIFFIN DONORS

Merilyn Sleigh &
Raoul de Ferranti
Kim Williams AM and
Catherine Dovey

Main Stage Donors
$5,000 - $9,999
Anonymous (1)
Antoniette Albert
Gil Appleton
Lisa Barker & Don Russell
Wendy Blacklock
Ellen Borda
Louise Christie
Bernard Coles
Lyndell & Daniel Droga
Danny Gilbert AM &
Kathleen Gilbert
Ken & Lilian Horler
Kiong Lee & Richard Funston
Lee Lewis & Brett Boardman
David Marr & Sebastian
Tesoriero
Catriona Morgan-Hunn
Don & Leslie Parsonage
Anthony Paull
Sue Procter
Geoff & Wendy Simpson
Danielle Smith &
Sean Carmody
Walking Up the Hill
Foundation

Final Draft Donors
$2,000-$4,999
Gae Anderson
Baly Douglass Foundation
Helen Bauer &
Helen Lynch AM
Marilyn & David Boyer
Iolanda Capodanno
Alan Colletti
Bryony & Tim Cox
Lachlan Edwards
Elizabeth Fullerton
Kathy Glass
Jocelyn Goyen
GRANTPIRRIE/privare
Libby Higgin
Roanne & John Knox
Carina G. Martin
Janet Manuell
John McCallum &
Jenny Nicholls
John Mitchell
David Nguyen
Chris Reed
Leslie Stern
Stuart Thomas
Tea Uglow
Richard Weinstein &
Richard Benedict

Workshop Donors
$1,000-$1,999
Anonymous (4)
Michael Barnes
Katrina Barter
Cheery & Peter Best
Andrew Bell & Joanna Bird
Christy Boyce &
Madeleine Beaumont
Keith Bradley AM
Michael & Charmaine Bradley
Dr Bernadette Brennan
Jane Bridge
Corinne & Bryan
Stephen & Annabelle Burley
Susan Carleton
Adrian Christie
Sally Crawford
Laura Crennan
Nathan Croft & James White
Cris Croker & David West
Jane Curry
Timothy Davis
Carol Dettman
T Dolland & S McComb
Sue and Jim Dominguez
Christine Dunstan
Bob Ernst
Ros & Paul Espie
Brian Everingham
John & Libby Fairfax
Rowena Falzon
Robyn Fortescue &
Rosie Wagstaff
Jennifer Giles
Nicky Gluyas
Melinda Graham
Peter Gray & Helen Thwaites
Reg Graycar
Sherry Gregory
Antonia Haralambis
Judge Joe Harman
Kate Harrison
James Hartwright &
Kerrin D'Arcy
Johh Head
Danielle Hoareau
Mark Hopkinson &
Michelle Opie
Susan Hyde
Ann Johnson
Margaret Johnston
Deborah Jones
David & Adrienne Kitching
Jennifer Ledgar & Bob Lim
Richard & Elizabeth Longes
Chris Marrable &
Kate Richardson
Jane Munro
Elaine & Bill McLaughlin
Dr Steve McNamara
Kent and Sandra McPhee
Joy Minter
Kate Mulvany
Tommy Murphy
John Nerthercoate
Ian Neuss & Penny Young
Patricia Novikoff
Ian Phipps
Martin Portus
Steve & Belinda Rankine
Sylvia Rosenblum
David & Dianne Russell
Sonia Simich
Jann Skinner
Geoffrey Starr
Robyn Stone
Adam Suckling &
Pip McGuinness
Margie Sullivan
Peter Talbot
Mike Thompson
Sue Thomson

GRIFFIN DONORS

Daniel P. Tobin
Janet Wahlquist
Simone Whetton
Rosemary White
Paul & Jennifer Winch
Elizabeth Wing
Kathy Zeleny

Reading Donors
$500-$999
Anonymous (3)
Brian Abel
Amity Alexander
Jes Andersen
Robyn Ayres
Melissa Ball
Nikki Barrett
Penny Beran
Cherry & Peter Best
Phillip Black
Anne Britton
Annie Bourke
Larry Boyd &
Barbara Caine AM
Simon Burke AO
Marianne Bush
Bill Calcraft
Gaby Carney
Jane Christensen
Amanda Clark
Eloise Curry
Melita Daru
David Davies
Michael Diamond
Max Dingle
Tim Duggan
David Earp
Wendy Elder
Leonie Flannery
Peter Graves
Tonkin Zulaikha Greer
Edwina Guinness
Stephanie & Andrew Harrison
Mary Holt
David Hoskins &
Paul McKnight
Sylvia Hrovatin
Marian & Nabeel Ibrahim
Mira Joksovic
David Jonas
Susan J Kath
Susan Kippax
Maruschka Loupis
Anne Loveridge
Ian & Elizabeth MacDonald
Robert Marks
Rebecca Massey
Christopher McCabe
Wendy McCarthy AO
Patrick McIntyre
Nicole McKenna
Paula McLean
Keith Miller
Stephen Mills
Neville Mitchell
Sarah Mort
William Peck
Carolyn Penfold
Judy Phillips
Malcolm Poole
Chris Puplick
David Purves
Jennifer Rani
Alex-Oonagh Redmond
Annabel Ritchie
Jonquil Ritter
Roslyn Renwick
Judith & Frank Robertson
Colleen Roche
Karen Rodgers & Bill Harris
Gemma Rygate
Rob & Rae Spence
Mary Stollery & Eric Dole
Catherine Sullivan &
Alexandra Bowen
Pearl Tan & Priya Roy
Ariadne Vromen
Jonathan Ware
John Waters
Rosemary White
William Zappa

First Draft Donors
$200-$499
Anonymous (8)
Nicole Abadee &
Rob Macfarlan
Susan Ambler
Elizabeth Antonievich
Barbara Armitage
William Armitage
Wendy Ashton
Chris Baker
Jan Barr
Edwina Birch
Rebecca Bourne Jones
Elizabeth Boyd
Shay Bristowe
Peter Brown
Dean Bryant & Mathew Frank
Wendy Buswell
Ruth Campbell
David Caulfield
Charlie Chan &
Angela Catterns
Peter Chapman
Sue Clark
Amanda Connelly
Brendan Crotty &
Darryl Toohey
Bryan Cutler
Owen Davies
Dora Den Hengst
Joanne & Sue Dalton
Susan Donnelly
Dr June Donsworth
Peter Duerden
Anna Duggan
Michele Dulcken
Kathy Esson
Elizabeth Evatt
Michael Eyers
Eamon Flack
Paul Fletcher
Helen Ford
Lee French
Matt Garrett
Sarah & Braith Gilchrist
Jock Given
Deane Golding
Thomas Gottlieb
Brenda Gottsche
Keith Gow
Hannah Grant
Virginia & Kieran Greene
Jo Grisard

GRIFFIN DONORS

Sue Hackett
Jennifer Hagan & Ron Blair
Glen Hamilton
Elizabeth Hanley
Carol Hargreaves
Raewyn Harlock
Grania Hickley
Stephanie Hui
Matthew Huxtable
C John Keightley
Maria Kelly
James Kelly & Beu Phuong
Catherine Kennedy
Penelope Latey
Peta Leemen
Karen Lee Smith
Antoinette Le Marchant
Caleb Lewis
Mark Lillis
Liz Locke
Norman Long
Dr Peter Louw
Carolyn Lowry
Anni Macdougall
Guillermo Martin
Katrina Matthews
Louise McDonald
Edward McGuiness
Duncan McKay
Ellen McLoughlin
Ian McMillan
Sarah Miller
Bruce Milthorpe
Julia Mitchell
Catherine Moore
Pam Morris
Mullinars Casting Consultants
Dian Neligan
Carolyn Newman
Gennie Nevinson & Vivian Manwaring
Anthony Ong
Sally Patten
Susheela Peres Da Costa
Peter Pezzutti
Meredith Phelps
Belinda Piggott &
David Ojerholm
Marion Potts
Christopher Powell
Janelle Prescott
Andrew Pringle
Virginia Pursell
Steve Riethoff
Thelma Roach
In memory of Katherine Robertson
Ann Rocca
Catherine Rothery
Kevin and Shirley Ryan
Sharryn Ryan
Emily Scanlan
Julianne Schultz
Julia Selby
Diana Simmonds
Bridget Smith
Vanda & Martin Smith
Camilla Strang
The Steiner Family
Augusta Supple
Margot Tanjutco
Mark & Susan Tennant
Jane Theau
Elizabeth Thompson
Stephen Thompson
Susan Tiffin
Lawrence Vaux
Richard Vickery
Christophe Vivien
Belinda Wallington
Erik van Werven
Deanna Weir
Jennifer White
Ruth Wilson
Margaret Winn
Greg Wood
Eve Wynhausen
Robert Yuen
Aviva Ziegler

We would also like to thank Peter O'Connell for his expertise, guidance and time.

Current as of October 7 2020

SPONSORS

Griffin would like to thank the following:

Government Supporters

Patron 2020 Season

Production Partner

GIRGENSOHN
FOUNDATION

2020 Season Sponsor

alphabet.

Griffin Award

Griffin Studio

Griffin Ambassadors & Artistic Associate Sponsor

Creative Partners

Company Lawyers

Company Sponsors

SATURDAY PAPER

Access Partner

DESIGNKINGCOMPANY

Griffin Theatre Company is assisted by the Australian Government through the Australia Council, its arts funding and advisory body; and the NSW Government through Create NSW.